Education in the 80's:

MULTIETHNIC EDUCATION

The Advisory Panel

MULTIETHNIC EDUCATION

James A. Banks
Editor
University of Washington, Seattle

Classroom Teacher Consultant
Barbara J. Shin
Pratt Continuous Progress Elementary School
Minneapolis, Minnesota

National Education Association
Washington, D. C.

Stock No. 3157–1–00 (paper)
           3158–X–00 (cloth)

Note

The opinions expressed in this publication should not be construed as representing the policy or position of the National Education Association. Materials published as part of the NEA Education in the 80's series are intended to be discussion documents for teachers who are concerned with specialized interests of the profession.

Library of Congress Cataloging in Publication Data
Main entry under title:

Education in the 80's—multiethnic education.

   (Education in the 80's)
   Bibliography: p.
   1. Minorities—Education—United States—Addresses, essays, lectures.
2. Intercultural education—United States—Addresses, essays, lectures.
I. Banks, James A.   II. Series.
LC3731.E38   371.97'0973   80–21710
ISBN 0–8106–3158–X
ISBN 0–8106–3157–1 (pbk.)

Contents

Editor

James A. Banks is Professor of Education at the University of Washington. Dr. Banks is a specialist in social studies education and multiethnic education. His books include *Teaching Strategies for the Social Studies, Teaching Strategies for Ethnic Studies, Black Self-Concept: Implications for Education and Social Science,* and *Multiethnic Education: Theory and Practice.*

Classroom Teacher Consultant

Barbara J. Shin is a teacher at the Pratt Continuous Progress Elementary School in Minneapolis, Minnesota. Ms. Shin was awarded an H. Councill Trenholm Memorial Award by NEA in 1979 for leadership in human relations education.

This is an informative and important book. It speaks cogently to the present and future educational needs of individuals, ethnic groups, and the nation. Creatively edited by James A. Banks, this book is a "futures" guide for every educator. It can serve as a useful guide for educational excellence sought by classroom teachers who have a commitment to become multiethnic educators, who are conscious of the nation's ethnic diversity, and who want ethnic pluralism to be reflected, supported, and respected in their classrooms.

This book will help teachers in multiethnic communities respond more effectively to the ethnic diversity within their classrooms and schools. It is also a useful and rational guide for teachers working in isolated monocultural communities who would like their students to attain the knowledge, attitudes, and skills needed to appreciate the ethnic diversity in the United States, and to improve or establish positive intergroup relations with members of other racial and ethnic groups.

The various chapters present fresh perspectives on our country's multiethnic experience and on the history of public education as it relates to the nation's ethnic groups, including research which has important implications for teaching and learning in diverse educational settings. Thus the book helps us realize that in collaboration with the larger society, we educators can assist in bringing about the reform and the excitement so desperately needed today in our public schools.

This book contains a combination of elements that teachers rarely find in one volume. It provides a philosophical background; a multiethnic, historical perspective; instructional guidelines; planning procedures; and important information about ways that other professionals, such as counselors and test specialists, can support our efforts to implement multiethnic educational reforms. Going beyond the four walls of the classroom, its concept of education includes the school and the community, as well as the popular media and other aspects of what Cortés perceptively calls "the societal curriculum." In other words, the contributors are not under the widespread illusion that *schooling* is the same as *education.*

Highlighting the need to examine the total educational environment when planning and implementing innovations such as multiethnic education, the authors point out that the school and the community must work cooperatively in the educational process. Efforts must be undertaken to bridge the gaps between the home, the school, and the community. As the authors indicate, however, the home, the school, and the community often distrust one another and contradict, rather than support, one another's purposes and goals. The distance between the societal and the school curricula—so clearly described by Cortés—is enhanced by behavioral specifics in Gay's description of the conflict between the home cultures of ethnic youths and the culture of the school. Cox and Ramírez describe the frequent conflict between the learning styles of ethnic youths and those favored by the school. And Grant discusses the benefits that can result from school-community collaboration, highlighting the need for home-school cooperation in order to effectively educate students.

Educators other than classroom teachers will also find this book useful and informative. Counselors, social workers, and administrators will be more sensitive and rational in performing their jobs and providing leadership in reforming the educational program to meet the challenge from the changing student enrollment if they absorb its ideas and begin to implement the policies and practices recommended. Administrators, in particular, must be aware of the strategies used by multiethnic teachers if they are to fulfill their supportive roles and effectively evaluate and encourage the teaching-learning process in pluralistic schools. But the key person is the classroom teacher. Teachers are the ones who make the difference. Working cooperatively with parents, the community, and our colleagues, we have the power to bring equity to the school environment for all students.

As a classroom teacher who works with a multiethnic and multiracial population, I have spent many years searching for educationally sound content and processes that will help bring equity into my classroom and school. Many readers have probably been engaged in similar quests. After reading this book, they will therefore understand more fully why I say this scholarly work summarizes years of research and readings for the classroom teacher. Each chapter succinctly captures the essence of an important issue or problem related to multiethnic education. The authors are trailblazers in this area, deeply committed to human rights and educational equity.

I hope that readers will find the learnings reflected in this book as renewing, reinforcing, and expanding as I have found them. For example, because I am a holistic and visual learner, I found Figure 2 in chapter 1 very meaningful. In this figure, James A. Banks identifies the scope of "The Total School Environment," which is discussed by the other authors, and by Banks himself in chapter 10. Indeed, every chapter contains specific helps for teachers as well as common threads that unite the book. Among these are behavioral references to which we can all relate. For example, in discussing an understanding of language diversity, Saville-Troike cites specific messages that students express, both verbally and nonverbally, that are influenced by ethnicity. Students' communication systems also influence the learning environment, since the way in which teachers perceive and respond to these communication styles significantly affects the learning process.

Baker provides insights into step-by-step planning behavior, explaining how teachers can change the curriculum to make it more multiethnic. Howard describes the implementation of an innovative and effective multiethnic education program within a predominantly White suburban community. His encouraging account should stimulate other teachers working in similar communities to take action to break down ethnic encapsulation and ethnocentrism. Gay focuses on the culturally determined behaviors that we can observe in the classroom, recommending an analysis of these behaviors to improve interpersonal relations between students and teachers.

Several of the writers observe that individuals respond to their ethnic cultures and characteristics differently. Thus, there are tremendous differences within ethnic groups. This observation has powerful implications for planning and teaching. Arciniega asks us to view ethnic identifications and group behaviors as positive coping behaviors to be fostered as sources of strength for students rather than as cultural deficits to be eradicated. Cherry A. Banks considers the awareness of ethnic cultures needed for effective interethnic interactions, and the way in which each individual's ethnic culture influences cross-cultural interactions and communications. As she points out, we are all individuals, yet members of groups. This theme of individuality and groupness is also a concern of ˌCortés in the "curriculum of personal experience."

Mercer's chapter on testing is enormously instructive. I have long been aware of the discrimination resulting from norm-referenced testing, and the way it perpetuates educational inequality with tracking and isolation under the guise of homogeneous grouping and its alleged benefits. Mercer's suggested alternative to such tests is equitable and should be helpful to most teachers.

In a chapter on the classroom teacher as the most important factor in the student's learning environment, Currie suggests guidelines for training teachers to function successfully in multiethnic educational settings. Cheng, Brizendine, and Oakes thoughtfully challenge several traditional assumptions about schooling in their discussion of the school in relation to the dominant ideologies and goals of society. And in the Afterword, Blumenberg highlights key points of the book, proposing actions needed by a variety of institutions to help implement reforms in multiethnic education. The bibliography which appears at the end of the book is a useful source of additional information on the issues, problems, and proposals for action presented in this publication.

As teachers, we have the future of multiethnic education precariously placed in our hands. The way we attend to and nurture it will determine its value to the education of a new clientele and to our society as a world leader. The complex problems facing the teaching profession today demand strong and concerted leadership for resolution. Let us be the ones to provide the leadership needed to revitalize our profession and to bring about educational equality for all the nation's youth. The reforms needed to implement multiethnic education provide teachers with a rich opportunity for leadership. This thoughtful and stimulating book issues a challenge. Let us accept it.

I am deeply grateful to James A. Banks and his colleagues for another fine contribution to the profession, and to the National Education Association for its continuing leadership in the ongoing quest for human rights and educational equity.

Barbara J. Shin, Teacher
Pratt Continuous Progress Elementary School
Minneapolis, Minnesota

The ethnic revitalization movements of the 1960's emerged in response to the inequality and institutionalized discrimination that American ethnic groups were experiencing. These movements in the United States echoed throughout the world as ethnic groups in such nations as Great Britain, Canada, and Australia renewed their quests for equality and deepened their expressions of cultural integrity and pride.

The ethnic revitalization movements caught both the established social science community and educational institutions by surprise. Social scientists, whose disciplines were dominated by assimilationist concepts and ideologies, lacked adequate concepts and theories to explain and analyze the new ethnic quests for separatism, identity, power, and equality. The nation's schools, colleges, and universities, which promoted Anglo-conformity goals and perspectives, lacked the knowledge, vision, and commitment needed to respond progressively to these movements.

Since the 1960's, with varying degrees of success and reflection, the nation's schools and other educational institutions have responded to the unique educational problems of the nation's growing ethnic populations. Many schools have also tried to increase the ethnic awareness of the Anglo-American population and help all the nation's students to become more sensitive to and knowledgeable about the racial and ethnic diversity in America. Professional educational associations, such as the National Council for the Social Studies, the Association for Supervision and Curriculum Development, the National Council of Teachers of English, and the American Association of Colleges for Teacher Education, have issued position statements, publications, and guidelines, and sponsored workshops, conferences, and institutes to support the emerging concepts of multiethnic and multicultural education. The National Education Association, the publisher of this book, has sponsored previous publications and projects related to ethnic and cultural diversity. Commercial textbook publishers have also published books and materials related to ethnic studies and multiethnic education.

These efforts by schools, professional education associations, and textbook publishers have, without question, had an impact on the nation's schools and colleges. The degree of impact is difficult to determine. Almost any educator who has recently visited schools in different parts of the nation would probably agree, however, that the teaching strategies, culture, norms, and other aspects of the schools indicate that many of the nation's educators have been little if at all influenced by the myriad developments and publications in multiethnic education.

The rise of neoconservatism, the so-called "back to the basics" movement, and the recent upsurge of racial incidents in the nation suggest that the national commitment to equality for excluded groups which emerged during the 1960's is rapidly waning and that many leaders would like to see the nation return to the "good old days" of doing business as usual, with little attention devoted to the problems and promises of ethnic group life in the United States.

The current national sociopolitical climate is a pernicious one in which to talk and write about multiethnic education in the 1980's. Many developments in the world, however, suggest that helping our future citizens develop cultural knowledge and global understandings of events and issues (both within this nation and in the rest of the world) may be our only hope for survival as a strong and respected nation in the next century. It is clear that the non-White nations of the world, such as those of the Arab world, Africa, and the People's Republic of China, will play key roles in determining public policy on such issues as energy and international politics that will deeply affect our lives and the role of the United States in the world community.

Anglo-centric schools that teach students distorted and restricted views of our nation and world, and that perpetuate ethnic ethnocentrism, cannot prepare effective and sensitive citizens for the world community of the future. A reform of the total school environment is therefore imperative. The school should reflect the ethnic and racial diversity in our nation and world, and help students develop the cultural knowledge and cross-cultural behavior needed for interpersonal and international survival and effective decisionmaking in the twenty-first century. Only a sound and thoughtful multiethnic education can prepare our students for the challenges of tomorrow's world.

The collection of essays in this book is designed to help teachers and other members of the educational community attain the insights and conceptual understandings needed to prepare American youths to function effectively within the world community of the present and the future. The book focuses on key conceptual variables in the school environment that need to be reformed so that schools may create environments in which students from all ethnic and racial groups can experience educational equity. Figure 2 in chapter 1 illustrates these variables. No attempt is made to survey the histories and cultures of specific ethnic groups since that is beyond the scope of this work. Several informative publications that accomplish this goal admirably already exist, and some of them are included in the annotated bibliography at the end of this book.

The reader may want to know why the term *multiethnic education* rather than *multicultural education* is used in the title of this book. Multiethnic education refers to the process used by educational institutions to reform their environments so that students from diverse ethnic and racial groups will experience educational equity. Multicultural education refers to a reform process whose aim is to create an educational environment in which a wide range of cultural groups, such as women, handicapped persons, ethnic groups, and various regional groups, will experience educational equity. Thus multicultural education is a much more comprehensive concept than multiethnic education, which is limited to the concerns and problems of racial and ethnic groups. Multiethnic education is therefore used in the title because this book's scope is limited to the research and educational concerns of racial and ethnic groups. Consequently, the book deals with but one very important part of the broader concept of multicultural education.

I am indebted to the gifted and knowledgeable professionals who took valuable time from their busy schedules to help with this publication. I am especially grateful to the authors of the chapters for their thoughtful and informative work. I also wish to thank the individuals (named elsewhere) who served as prepublication reviewers. Their perceptive comments on the manuscript enabled us to strengthen it. It was in response to the comments of one reviewer that I added the previously published chapters by Cheng and his colleagues and by Currie to broaden the scope of this volume. While the reviews were helpful and informative, the authors and the editor assume total responsibility for the contents.

James A. Banks, Editor
University of Washington, Seattle

CHAPTER 1

The Nature of Multiethnic Education

James A. Banks

America has long been a land rich in ethnic diversity. Before the European colonists began to arrive in the fifteenth century, many different groups of Native Americans—with varied cultures, languages, and physical characteristics—lived on the continent. Then the Spaniards, the French, and the English established colonies in North America. Africans came with the earliest Spanish explorers. The physical and cultural mixture of these diverse racial and ethnic groups further enriched pluralism in America. New cultures and ethnic groups, such as Mexican-Americans and Afro-Americans, emerged.

During the colonial period many different European ethnic and nationality groups came across the vast Atlantic to improve their economic status, pulled by the promise of the American dream widespread in Europe and pushed by the harsh conditions and political repression in their homelands. Each of these European groups tried to establish European institutions on American soil and to remake North America in the image of its native land. The British, however, became the dominant and most powerful ethnic group in early colonial America, controlling entry to most social, economic, and political institutions.[1] Immigrants from other nations—the French Huguenots, the Irish, the Scotch-Irish, and the Germans—were unable to fully participate in colonial life and culture and became victims of overt discrimination as the attainment of Anglo characteristics became a requisite for full societal participation. Thus the groundwork was laid for Americanization to become synonymous with Anglicization.

THE MELTING POT IDEOLOGY

Like other social institutions, the public schools were dominated by Anglo-Saxon Protestant culture and values. One of their major functions was to rid students of their ethnic characteristics and to make them culturally Anglo-Saxons. Thus the schools taught the children of immigrants contempt for their cultures, forcing them to experience self-alienation and self-rejection. Many immigrant parents accepted and promoted Anglo-Saxon behavior and values because they believed that Anglicization was necessary for their survival and for their children's economic and social mobility. As Greenbaum observes, the immigrants accepted Anglo-Saxon values and Anglicization because of *shame* and *hope:*

> Most important is the fact that the main fuel for the American melting pot was *shame.* The immigrants were best instructed in how to repulse themselves; millions of people were taught to be ashamed of their own faces, their family names, their parents and grandparents, and their class patterns, histories, and life outlooks. This shame had incredible power to make us learn, especially when coupled with *hope,* the other main energy source for the melting pot —hope about becoming modern, about being secure, about escaping the wars and depressions of the old country, and about being equal with the old Americans.[2]

The melting pot ideology, popularized by the English Jewish author, Israel Zangwill, thus became the philosophical justification for the cultural and ethnic desocialization promoted by the society and the schools. All European cultures, it was argued, were to be blended, and from them a novel and superior culture would emerge. Melting pot advocates rarely discussed non-White ethnic groups such as Blacks and Indians. Perhaps they assumed that these ethnic groups would stick to the bottom of the mythical melting pot. In some ways, however, the Anglo-conformity concept more accurately describes what happened to ethnic and immigrant groups in America than the melting pot idea. Ethnic and immigrant groups abandoned major parts of their cultures and acquired many of the values, behaviors, and characteristics of Anglo-Saxon Protestants. But neither the Anglo-conformity nor the melting pot concept adequately describes the complex process which occurred and is still occurring in the development of American civilization and culture.

Both concepts are in some ways incomplete and/or misleading because non-Anglo ethnic groups have had (and are still having) a much more cogent impact on American society than is reflected by either theory. Anglo-Saxon Protestant culture in the United States has been greatly influenced by other ethnic and immigrant cultures. Such ethnic groups as Italian-Americans and Polish-Americans retain many more ethnic characteristics than is often acknowledged and/or recognized. The rather strong ethnic cultures existing within many Black and Chicano communities are usually more often recognized by scholars and practitioners. As Novak has insightfully pointed out, however, ethnicity within White ethnic communities is often subconscious and subtle.[3] Ethnic individuals themselves, especially White ethnic group members, are often unaware of the extent to which they are ethnic. As early as 1963, Glazer and Moynihan recognized the tenacity of ethnicity within modern American society, writing in their classic book, *Beyond the Melting Pot,* "Individuals, in very considerable numbers to be sure, broke out of their mold, but the groups remained. . . . The point about the melting pot is that it did not happen."[4]

THE LIMITATIONS OF EXISTING CONCEPTS AND IDEOLOGIES

The melting pot concept is inaccurate and misleading because human cultures are complex and dynamic and do not melt like iron. The Anglo-conformity concept suggests that Anglo-Saxon Protestants were changed very little in America and that other ethnic groups did all the changing. This theory does not reflect the fact that while Anglo-Saxon Protestants were influencing other ethnic groups, these groups were also influencing the values, behaviors, and characteristics of Anglo-Saxons.

In the 1960's, the idea of cultural pluralism became popular in the educational literature. This idea was born near the turn of the century when tremendous numbers of European immigrants were entering the United States, at the same time that nativism, designed to stop the massive flow of immigrants, was becoming pernicious and widespread.[5] A few philosophers and writers, such as Horace Kallen, Randolph Bourne, and Julius Drachsler, strongly defended the rights of the immigrants, arguing that they had a right to maintain their ethnic cultures and institutions in the United States, and using the concepts of *cultural pluralism* and *cultural democracy* to describe their philosophical positions.

During the 1960's, many members of ethnic groups such as Blacks, Mexican-Americans, and American Indians endorsed some form of cultural pluralism. An idea born near the turn of the century was thus refashioned to fit the hopes, aspirations, and dreams of alienated ethnic peoples more than half a century later. Like the concepts of Anglo-conformity and the melting pot, however, cultural pluralism does not adequately describe the complex nature of ethnic relations and cultural development in the United States.

In its strongest form, the cultural pluralist idea suggests that ethnic groups live within tight ethnic boundaries and communities and rarely, if ever, participate within the universal American culture and society. This concept denies the reality of a universal American culture and national identity which every American, regardless of ethnicity and ethnic group membership, shares to a large extent. Most Americans highly value their national identity, even though they may have a strong sense of ethnic identity and significant ethnic behaviors and characteristics. This common national culture and identity should be recognized, respected, and promoted by the schools in any reform effort related to ethnicity. The *conceptualization* of the shared American culture and identity, however, should be broadened to more accurately reflect the ethnic, racial, and cultural diversity in our nation. For example, Afro-Americans, Mexican-Americans, and Puerto Ricans in the United States usually do not find their cultural expressions, hopes, aspirations, and problems depicted in many of the media and school presentations of the *American* culture and the *American* ways of life.

THE NEED FOR A NEW CONCEPT AND IDEOLOGY TO GUIDE SCHOOL REFORM

To design sound multiethnic school programs, we need a conceptualization of ethnic groups in the United States which accurately reflects the complex nature of ethnicity in America. Some writers argue, for example, that the United States is an *Anglo society,* their argument emanating from the assumption that American culture developed as the Anglo-conformity concept suggests. If the United States is considered an Anglo society, then *American* literature is *Anglo-American* literature and *American* history is *Anglo-American* history. The schools, the media, and other American institutions have traditionally assumed this. *But our nation is not an Anglo nation culturally, even though Anglo-Saxon Protestants exercise the major social, economic, and political power in the United States.*

However, many presentations of American culture and society in

18

the mass media, in textbooks (which have improved considerably in recent years), and in the school curriculum depict the United States in ways which suggest or give the impression that American culture and Anglo-American culture are synonymous. For example, Alistair Cooke's *America,* both the television program and the popular book that followed, depicts the United States primarily as a nation of Anglo-Americans and their culture. We urgently need new views about America and ethnicity to permeate the school as well as other institutions. Only when they have been helped to gain new concepts about *America* and the role of ethnicity in our society, will teachers be able to function effectively within classrooms which promote positive norms toward the differences within our society. If schools are to help this nation shape the kind of future which is imperative for our survival in the twenty-first century, they must help students gain broader and more accurate views of American society and culture.

MULTIPLE ACCULTURATION: A NEW CONCEPT

According to Gordon, *structural pluralism* best describes the ethnic reality in the United States. He believes that ethnic groups in America have experienced gross levels of cultural assimilation but the nation is characterized by structural pluralism.[6] In other words, ethnic groups are highly culturally assimilated but have separate ethnic subsocieties, such as Black fraternities, Jewish social clubs, and Chicano theaters.

Although Gordon's concept deals more adequately with the complexity of ethnic diversity in American society than Anglo-conformity, the melting pot, or cultural pluralism, structural pluralism needs to be combined with another concept, *multiple acculturation,*[7] to completely and accurately describe the past and present formation of the universal American culture. The White Anglo-Saxon Protestant culture in America was changed as were the cultures of Africans and of Asian immigrants. African cultures influenced and changed the WASP culture as the WASP culture influenced and modified African and Asian cultures. What we experienced, and what we are still experiencing, is *multiple acculturation* and not a kind of unidirectional assimilation whereby the Black culture was influenced by the WASP culture but the latter was not influenced by the former. The general or universal culture in the United States resulted from this series of multiple acculturations. Anglo-Saxon Protestant culture had the greatest influence on the development of American civilization and culture. *However, other ethnic groups, such as Blacks, Jews, and Chicanos, have cogently influenced the universal American culture much more than is often recognized.* These groups have strongly affected

American music, English, literature, values, and behavioral patterns. Their contributions to the economy and to labor have also been substantial.

THE NATURE OF AMERICAN CULTURE

American culture consists of a shared universal culture as well of ethnic subsocieties and communities (see Figure 1). The universal American culture resulted (and is resulting) from ethnic cultural elements which have become universalized and cultural components which resulted from the synthesis of ethnic cultural elements and cultural elements which evolved within this nation. This culture is shared by all the ethnic groups in the United States. The ethnic subsocieties

FIGURE 1
ETHNIC SUBSOCIETIES AND THE UNIVERSAL AMERICAN SOCIETY

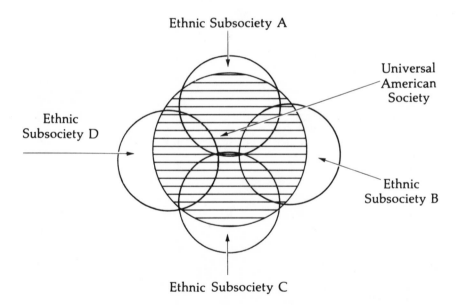

This figure represents the universal American society by the ruled area. This culture is shared by all ethnic groups within the United States. A, B, C, and D represent ethnic subsocieties consisting of unique ethnic institutions, values, and cultural elements which are nonuniversalized and are shared primarily by members of specific ethnic groups.

within the nation consist of nonuniversalized ethnic cultural elements and institutions. These are still shared primarily by ethnic subgroups. Almost every American participates both within the universal American culture and society as well as within his or her ethnic subsociety.

THE MULTIETHNIC IDEOLOGY: IMPLICATIONS FOR SCHOOL REFORM

My analysis of ethnicity in American society leads to a philosophical position which may be called the multiethnic ideology, since one of its key assertions is that Americans function within several cultures, including the mainstream culture and various ethnic subcultures. This multiethnic ideology suggests that a major goal of school reform for the future should be to help students develop cross-cultural competency, consisting of the skills, attitudes, and abilities needed to function within their own ethnic subsociety and the universal American culture, as well as within and across different ethnic cultures (see chapter 10).

Historically, the school has alienated ethnic youths from their ethnic cultures and often has not succeeded in helping them acquire the skills and abilities needed to function within the mainstream American culture or within other ethnic communities. A major assumption undergirding the chapters in this book is that the school, in order to plan effectively for the future, must examine its assimilationist ideology and Anglo-Saxon goals, and structure an ideology and goals more consistent with the complex nature of ethnicity within American society. The multiethnic ideology is an appropriate one to guide school reform within a democratic pluralistic nation. To create a school environment consistent with this ideology requires systemic (or total) school reform.

Educators who want their schools to reflect a multiethnic ideology must examine their total school environment to determine the extent to which it is monoethnic and Anglo-centric, and then take appropriate steps to create and sustain a multiethnic educational environment. Initial school reform may focus on any one of several factors: school policy and politics, the ethnic and racial composition of the school staff, its attitudes and perceptions, the formalized and hidden curriculum, the learning styles and cultural behavioral patterns favored by the school, the teaching strategies and materials, the testing and counseling program, the languages and dialects sanctioned by the school, and the role of the community in the school. Figure 2 illustrates the total school environment, including these and other variables which must be reformed in order to make the school multiethnic.

FIGURE 2
TOTAL SCHOOL ENVIRONMENT

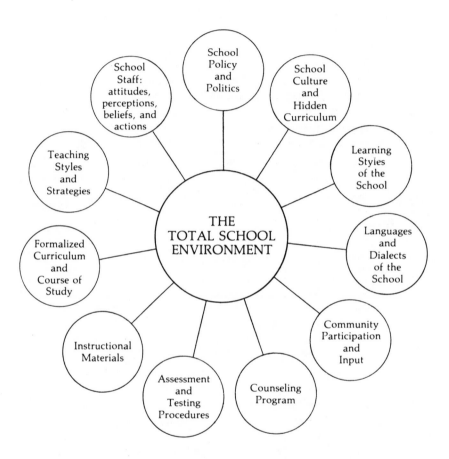

This figure conceptualizes the total school environment as a system consisting of a number of major identifiable variables and factors, such as school culture, school policy and politics, and formalized curriculum and course of study. In the idealized multiethnic school, each of these variables reflects ethnic pluralism. While any one of these factors may be the focus of initial school reform, changes must take place in each of them to create and sustain an effective multiethnic educational environment.

This book is conceptualized around this systemic (total) view of school reform. Each deals with an important part of the school or community environment which must be reformed in order to make the school more consistent with the culturally diverse and global nature of our nation and world. Pluralistic schools will help students enrich their personal and public lives and live more effectively within an increasingly small and interdependent world society.

REFERENCES

1. Maldwyn Allen Jones, *American Immigration* (Chicago: University of Chicago Press, 1960).

2. William Greenbaum, "America in Search of a New Ideal: An Essay on the Rise of Pluralism," *Harvard Educational Review* 44 (August 1974): 431.

3. Michael Novak, "Cultural Pluralism for Individuals: A Social Vision," in *Pluralism in a Democratic Society,* eds. Melvin M. Tumin and Walter Plotch (New York: Praeger Publishers, 1977), pp. 25–57.

4. Nathan Glazer and Daniel P. Moynihan, *Beyond the Melting Pot: The Negroes, Puerto Ricans, Jews, Italians, and Irish of New York City* (Cambridge, Mass.: M.I.T. Press, 1963), p. 290.

5. John Higham, *Strangers in the Land: Patterns of American Nativism 1860–1925* (New York: Atheneum, 1972).

6. Milton M. Gordon, *Assimilation in American Life* (New York: Oxford University Press, 1964).

7. I first presented the concept of *multiple acculturation* in James A. Banks, "Ethnicity: Implications for Curriculum Reform," *Social Studies* 70 (January–February 1979): 3–10; and in James A. Banks, "Shaping the Future of Multicultural Education," *Journal of Negro Education* 48 (Summer 1979): 237–52.

CHAPTER 2

The Societal Curriculum: Implications for Multiethnic Education

Carlos E. Cortés

Schools do not monopolize multiethnic education nor will they do so in the future, even if they so wish. Why? Because all students, all people, continuously receive multiethnic education—both positive and negative—outside schools. Aware of it or not, we are all students of the societal curriculum.

What is the societal curriculum? It is that massive, ongoing, informal curriculum of family, peer groups, neighborhoods, churches, organizations, occupations, mass media, and other socializing forces that "educate" all of us throughout our lives. Much of this informal education concerns ethnicity and ethnic groups.[1]

The recognition of the inevitability, omnipresence, and continuous pervasiveness of the multiethnic societal curriculum raises significant questions for both society in general and educators in particular. What does this curriculum "teach" about ethnicity? How does it affect what people "know" about ethnicity and ethnic groups? How does it influence beliefs, perceptions, attitudes, and behavior related to different ethnic groups? How does it increase or limit the effectiveness of school multiethnic education? What are its implications for schools, including school curriculum development? How can educators more effectively use it in school multiethnic education?

COMPONENTS OF THE SOCIETAL CURRICULUM

The multiethnic societal curriculum comprises at least four general components: (1) home, peer group, and neighborhood; (2) organizations and institutions; (3) the media; and (4) personal interethnic experiences. For each person, some aspects of that curriculum work positively to increase sensitivity to and understanding about ethnic groups. For each person, other aspects have a negative impact through spreading distortions, building stereotypes, or increasing prejudice. For example, studies have shown that many children develop well-formed attitudes about ethnic people, including prejudices and stereotypes, by the time they reach school.[2] While we have no way of determining the specific content of each person's individual societal curriculum, educators should remain alert to the general processes and diverse content of societal curriculum multiethnic education.

For most people, multiethnic education begins in the home, long before they enter school—through conversations about ethnic people or ethnic groups, through offhand remarks (including ethnic epithets and stereotyping), and through observation of actions of family members and friends. Multiethnic education also comes from the neighborhood peer group through conversations and the spreading of children's "knowledge" about ethnic groups. These statements do not label the home and the neighborhood multiethnic educational villains; they describe a reality. In fact, the family and the neighborhood may provide *either* or *both* positive or negative multiethnic education, even if not conscious that they are doing so.

Societal institutions and organizations other than schools and mass media institutions also serve as multiethnic educators. These include such institutions as churches, social clubs, political organizations, occupational associations, even the workplace itself. Each organization "educates," in such ways as providing religious and moral instruction, informing members of societal developments affecting their livelihoods, or exhorting members to take certain positions on issues. Some of this education may relate clearly to multiethnic concerns; other aspects may have less obvious, but no less significant, ethnic implications.

A few specific examples of the ongoing institutional multiethnic curriculum include labor unions counseling members about undocumented aliens and minority job training programs; religious leaders delivering sermons about desegregation; professional associations discussing affirmative action; private businesses or government agencies providing cultural awareness training for their employees; and social clubs maintaining ethnically oriented membership policies.

The media—television, motion pictures, radio, newspapers, and magazines—rank among the most powerful and pervasive aspects of the societal curriculum.[3] Television, for example, has been receiving increasing scholarly attention. One study reported that young people between the ages of 3 and 16 spend one-sixth of their waking hours with the television set.[4] By the time of graduation, the average high school senior will have spent 12,000 hours in the classroom and 15,000 hours in front of the television set, according to another estimate.

Some examples of the multiethnic educational impact of the so-called entertainment media include the following. In a pioneering study, Ruth C. Peterson and L. L. Thurstone discovered that viewing the classic silent film *Birth of a Nation* increased student prejudice toward Black Americans.[5] Irwin C. Rosen found that the film *Gentleman's Agreement* improved student attitudes toward Jews, even though most of the students tested stated that the film *had not* changed their attitudes.[6] A more recent study reported that White children felt that TV comedies like "The Jeffersons" and "Sanford and Son" accurately portrayed Black family life, although these same children admitted that such shows contrasted with personal experiences with their own Black friends, whom they labeled as exceptions.[7] A teacher in one of my multiethnic education courses discovered that her elementary school students had deeply rooted preconceptions about gypsies. In discussing where they had "learned" so much, students responded with answers ranging from "my folks" to "Wolfman" movies! These examples provide evidence of both the actual and potential multiethnic educational impact of the media.

Finally, of course, is the curriculum of personal experience. Increasing national mobility has drastically reduced the possibility of living in total ethnic isolation. Most people have some sort of personal interethnic contact—in school, on the job, through travel, or in their communities. Personal experiences vary, as do the ways in which they are perceived, interpreted, reacted to, and remembered. Yet these experiences comprise an important part of each person's multiethnic societal curriculum and become integrated into the personal storehouse of multiethnic knowledge and attitudes.

TOWARD UNDERSTANDING OR MISUNDERSTANDING

The societal curriculum has both positive and negative multiethnic effects. Good interethnic personal experiences can increase positive perceptions of other ethnic groups; negative experiences can create or reinforce prejudice. Some families make a conscious effort to bring multiethnic understanding into the home, provide positive interethnic experiences, and avoid ethnic slurs and stereotyping; other families take the opposite tack, leaving a terrible legacy for our society in terms of interethnic misunderstanding.

Businesses and government agencies which provide training in intercultural understanding serve as positive multiethnic educational forces; those which ignore this need or implement procedures and practices which discriminate, *however unintentionally,* against persons of certain ethnic backgrounds make multiethnic negativism a part of their day-to-day curriculum. By showing "The Autobiography of Miss Jane Pittman," "Roots", and "Holocaust," television probably contributed to multiethnic understanding. Theatrical and television films ranging from traditional anti-Native American westerns to the recent plague of ethnic gang movies, however, have helped to heighten interethnic fears, distrust, and stereotyping.

For better or for worse, the multiethnic societal curriculum has had and will continue to have a powerful educational influence. Moreover, whether because of neglect or ineffectiveness of multiethnic education, schools have not successfully offset the negative aspects of the societal curriculum. In fact, as analyses of ethnic content of textbooks and children's stories have demonstrated, schools may contribute in some respects toward interethnic negativism.[8] In a recent social studies assessment project of the California State Department of Education, seventh grade students in 65 California public schools were asked to select one of four answers to "Which of the following is an example of an ethnic group in the United States?" Fourteen percent selected "The United Auto Workers," 24 percent each answered "All the people who live in the same town" and "The Chinese," and 34 percent answered "People on welfare"! The societal curriculum had done its job.

INTEGRATING THE SOCIETAL CURRICULUM INTO THE SCHOOL CURRICULUM

When designing and implementing multiethnic education, educators should constantly and seriously consider the societal curriculum. To ignore it is to operate in a land of make-believe, because students will learn about ethnicity and ethnic groups from the societal curriculum and that learning will affect their school multiethnic education. I would suggest at least two basic lines of educational reform. First, integrate the multiethnic societal curriculum into the school curriculum. Second, attempt to make the societal curriculum a more positive multiethnic educator.

There are myriad ways to integrate the societal curriculum into the school curriculum. I will discuss three of these strategies: (1) building from student "knowledge," (2) studying the local community, and (3) bringing media into the classroom.

One of my favorite strategies is to build from preexistent student beliefs. Prior to teaching about a particular ethnic group in school, have students keep records of the ways in which they have observed the societal curriculum "teaching" about that group—through personal experiences, neighborhood, media, and other institutions. Such an approach will help raise student awareness of the existence and content of the societal curriculum as well as of their own particular beliefs. Moreover, this strategy can "prime" students for the classroom study of the group by helping educators avoid what philosopher Paul Tillich has labeled one of the basic failings of education—"to throw answers like stones at the heads of those who have not yet asked the questions." Most important, this approach can contribute to preparing students for a lifetime of continuous understanding of the multiethnic societal curriculum.

A second strategy is to use the local community as a source of study. Effective multiethnic education requires expanding the classroom beyond four walls. Every human being is a valuable source of knowledge. There are no class, caste, educational, or linguistic qualifications for being a part of history, for having a culture, for participating in society, for having family or ethnic group traditions, for perceiving the surrounding community, or for relating one's experiences.

Teachers can use various means to involve students in community study. For example, in the early elementary grades, persons of different ethnic backgrounds can be brought into the classroom to talk about their experiences, cultures, traditions, and beliefs. For older students, teachers can use field trips into local ethnic areas, student "cultural mapping" of the area around the school, and individual or team investigation into the historical development of local ethnic communities.

The writing of biographies of local individuals or families, including one's own, combines the development of research and writing skills with the discovery of personal or community roots.[9] This strategy may provide some students with their first in-depth personal contact with persons of different ethnic backgrounds. By hearing history and obtaining perspectives on society as viewed, recalled, and interpreted by persons of diverse ethnic backgrounds, students should obtain new and broader multiethnic perspectives on the U.S. past and the community around them.

Using these classroom interviews, field trips, community investigations, and family biographies as basic sources, teachers can help students test hypotheses, reevaluate previous conceptions (or misconceptions), and develop new generalizations about ethnic groups. Moreover, this process of community investigation can both increase interpersonal communication skills and give students a localized awareness of and sensitivity to the ethnic backgrounds in the community. Finally, community investigation can "humanize" the study of ethnicity for students by providing direct involvement in the workings of society.

A third strategy is to make multiethnic analysis of media an integral part of the K–12 curriculum. Feature films, radio, television, newspapers, magazines, and advertising can be stimulating and significant aspects of the school curriculum. So what's new? Haven't such sources been used for years in the classroom? Certainly, but seldom as sources for multiethnic analysis.

Too often the visual media, in particular, have served simply as surrogate teachers, as substitutes for the written word, or as spoken textbooks from which students are asked to recall factually and memorize uncritically. Media should not be viewed as transmitters of information, providers of facts, and pipelines of truth. Rather, they should be used as sources to be considered analytically, including an examination of their multiethnic perspectives, interpretations, and implications. How have different media portrayed, treated, or depicted different ethnic groups? What assumptions about ethnic groups and ethnicity do different media reflect? What historical forces and societal conditions have influenced media treatment of ethnicity during different eras?

In the early elementary grades, teachers can use children's stories about different ethnic groups as well as photographs, drawings, and animated films which include ethnic groups to introduce the concept of image formation. Advertisements in magazines and newspapers, on television, and even on billboards and bumper stickers, can be used throughout the elementary grades for the analysis of role depiction of ethnic groups.[10] The secondary school teacher may ask students to analyze the local newspaper or local or national news telecasts for the kinds of stories carried about specific ethnic groups and the interpretations of and attitudes toward ethnicity-related issues, such as immigration and desegregation. Feature films, television entertainment series, and newscasts make excellent classroom sources—not for what they "tell" about ethnicity, ethnic groups, or intergroup relations, but for the examination of the perspectives and interpretations they present. The goal, of course, is to raise the level of critical thinking and awareness of the process of media multiethnic education.[11]

CHANGING THE SOCIETAL CURRICULUM

While multiethnicizing the school curriculum, educators should also strive to help the societal curriculum become more of an ally and less of an antagonist in our multiethnic quest. While our ability to modify the societal curriculum is limited, there are avenues to effect change. Let me give some examples from my own experience.

Some of the most rewarding multiethnic education workshops have been for school district parents. In these workshops I not only explain and illustrate multiethnic education, but also suggest how parents can contribute multiethnically. Parents can be an extraordinary force for interethnic understanding—or misunderstanding. To maximize multiethnic educational effectiveness, school districts should make parent participation an integral part of their total program.

Societal institutions can be outstanding allies in the effort for multiethnic understanding. At the present time I am working with one religious denomination in developing a multiethnic approach to church school education using the theme, the Bible as a multicultural document. Educators should encourage governmental agencies to expand awareness training to help employees more effectively provide equitable services to persons of all ethnic and cultural backgrounds.

Many private businesses are introducing forms of multiethnic education into their employee development programs, a trend we should support. For example, at the present time, I am presenting a series of workshops on Mexican-Americans for supervisors and managers of Southern California companies. Why? Because of growing private industry awareness that the traditional "culture-blind" managerial training is merely "blind"—it does not necessarily prepare, and in some cases may actually disprepare, people to deal effectively and sensitively with a multiethnic work force and public.

IMPLICATIONS FOR TEACHER EDUCATION

Effective multiethnic education requires effective multiethnic teachers—teachers with multiethnic knowledge, skills, and attitudes. Such effectiveness ultimately requires the multiethnicizing of teacher education, both pre-service and in-service. This includes education in the multiethnic societal curriculum. Two strategies are the use of societal curriculum journals and training in multiethnic analysis of media.

Whenever I present in-service training courses, I ask each teacher to keep a multiethnic societal curriculum journal—a record of the education on ethnicity each observes outside school. Even those teachers possessing considerable awareness usually express surprise about the degree of multiethnic education occurring in the societal curriculum. "Awareness training," which helps teachers develop a better understanding of the societal influences on their own and their students' beliefs and attitudes about ethnicity and ethnic groups, should become an integral part of teacher education.

A second component of teacher education should be training in multiethnic analysis of media. In the spring of 1979, for example, Dr. Leon Campbell and I presented A Filmic Approach to Race and Ethnicity in the History of the Americas as one of the series of film-and-history courses offered at the University of California, Riverside. In that course we paired two feature films about three ethnic groups—a U.S. film and a Cuban film about Blacks in their respective societies, a U.S. film and a Bolivian film about the Indian experience in the two countries, and a U.S. film and an Argentine film about Italian-descent people in their nations. Students not only analyzed the treatment of ethnic groups and interethnic relations in the films, but they also investigated the historical and societal factors affecting those filmic interpretations. In addition, they wrote papers comparing class films with others viewed in the societal curriculum. The result—a growth in both general critical thinking and specific understanding of the multiethnic educational nature of the media.[12]

CONCLUSION

Schools exist to prepare young people for the future. Throughout that future, students will constantly "go to school" in the multiethnic societal curriculum. How they perceive that curriculum, how it affects their beliefs and attitudes, how it influences their interethnic behavior will to a great extent be a result of school successes or failures in preparing them to be multiethnically literate.[13]

How well are schools preparing students to deal with that curriculum—to be aware of it, to comprehend it, to analyze it, and to resist its more noxious effects? By helping students develop a knowledge base for a multiethnic societal curriculum, teachers will be preparing a citizenry that is more aware, sensitive, and constructive. As a result, our nation and the increasingly interdependent earth will be a better society.

REFERENCES

1. For example, see Randall M. Miller, ed., *The Kaleidoscopic Lens: Ethnic Images in American Film* (Englewood, N.J.: Jerome S. Ozer, 1979); and Cherry A. McGee Banks, "A Content Analysis of the Treatment of Black Americans on Television," *Social Education* 41, no. 4 (April 1977): 336–39, 344.

2. Mary Ellen Goodman, *Race Awareness in Young Children,* 2d ed. rev. (New York: Macmillan, 1964).

3. The Payne Fund Studies, published by Macmillan Company from 1933 through 1935, constitute one of the most extensive assessments of the impact of films on attitudes and behavior. In 1975, social psychologist George Comstock identified 2,300 research papers on television and human behavior (G. A. Comstock and M. L. Fisher, *Television and Human Behavior: A Guide to the Pertinent Scientific Literature* [Santa Monica, Calif.: Rand Corporation, 1975]).

4. Wilbur Schramm, Jack Lyle, and Edwin B. Parker, *Television in the Lives of our Children* (Stanford, Calif.: Stanford University Press, 1961), p. 30.

5. Ruth C. Peterson and L. L. Thurstone, *Motion Pictures and the Social Attitudes of Children* (New York: Macmillan, 1933), pp. 35–38.

6. Irwin C. Rosen, "The Effect of the Motion Picture 'Gentleman's Agreement' on Attitudes Toward Jews," *Journal of Psychology* 26 (1948): 525–36.

7. Bradley S. Greenberg, "Children's Reactions to TV Blacks," *Journalism Quarterly* 49 (Spring 1972): 5–14.

8. For example, see Michael Kane, *Minorities in Textbooks: A Study of Their Treatment in Social Studies Texts* (Chicago: Quadrangle Books, 1970).

9. David Weitzmann, *My Backyard History Book* (Boston: Little, Brown and Co., 1975).

10. James D. Cullery and Rex Bennett, "Selling Women, Selling Blacks," *Journal of Communication* 26 (Autumn 1976): 160–74.

11. Carlos E. Cortés, "The Role of Media in Multicultural Education," *Viewpoints in Teaching and Learning* 56 (Winter 1980), pp. 38–49.

12. For suggestions for teaching about race and ethnicity with feature films, see Carlos E. Cortés and Leon G. Campbell, *Race and Ethnicity in the History of the Americas: A Filmic Approach* (Riverside: Latin American Studies Program, University of California, 1979). I wish to thank the University of California, Riverside, for an Intramural Research Grant which supported this research.

13. James A. Banks, "Teaching Ethnic Literacy: A Comparative Approach," *Social Education* 27 (December 1973): 738–50.

CHAPTER 3

The Teacher and Multiethnic Education

Gwendolyn C. Baker

Multiethnic education as defined and presented by James A. Banks, the editor of this publication, is an encompassing concept. Consequently, developing an appropriate environment for its implementation has implications for every facet of the educational setting. First of all, the future of multiethnic education depends on the ability of all who are involved in the educational arena to assume the appropriate level of responsibility—state boards of education initiating and helping develop legislation to give direction to individual school systems; local school boards developing policy to provide support for the local school districts; superintendents playing an important role in the administrative aspects of implementation on a districtwide basis; and principals ensuring that the intent of the legislation and the policy are carried out at the building level. If and when these conditions are present, the success of multiethnic education in our schools is imminent; because, then, teachers will have the necessary support system to ensure successful implementation. Accordingly, with such a support system in place, the degree to which multiethnic education becomes a reality in our schools depends largely upon the attitude and behavior of the teacher. Indeed, the role and the responsibility of the teacher are crucial in determining the future and the success of multiethnic education.

SIGNIFICANCE OF TEACHER ATTITUDES AND BEHAVIOR

Teachers play a significant role in the formation of childrens' attitudes. Research suggests that next to parents, they are the most significant people in children's lives.[1] Thus the burden placed upon teachers is great. For example, children bring biases and prejudices to the classroom. Studies have found that they come to school with previously established negative attitudes about people who are different from themselves. When this happens, it becomes necessary for teachers to help change these existing attitudes and to encourage the children to develop accurate and positive images of such people.[2,3,4] If this cannot be done, our entire educational system must share the responsibility for propagating a monocultural view of society that is inconsistent with the past and present realities of life in the United States.[5] As long as the educational system is based on direct and frequent contact between teacher and child, the teacher's role is crucial in the success or failure of desired changes in the curriculum.[6] Therefore, teacher education and training are of the utmost importance.

Teachers, too, bring to the classroom biases and prejudices toward people who are different from themselves. These predispositions can influence the communication of accurate and objective information about ethnic groups in the educational setting. In addition, many teachers may lack factual information about ethnic group history, and religious and cultural diversity. This is not surprising because teachers, too, are the products of their education and training, and the majority have not been exposed to multiethnic education.

Of equal importance is the teacher's commitment to the value, the worth, and the dignity of every child in the classroom. The way in which the teacher acts out the way he/she feels will set the pattern for students.[7] Behavior is as important as attitude because it demonstrates the attitude. Therefore the teacher's behavior will reflect the teacher's feeling about the child. A sensitivity to the various cultures or ethnic groups and an acceptance of the viability of these diverse lifestyles are also necessary before information about them can be taught.

Multiethnic education implies the utilization of a multiethnic approach to the curriculum, an approach that involves planning and organizing the learning experiences for children in educational settings that will reflect ethnic and cultural diversity. It is therefore important for teachers, through classroom instruction, to develop attitudes and behavior conducive to living in a pluralistic society.

TEACHER PREPARATION

As indicated, the role and responsibility of the teacher are important aspects of multiethnic education, requiring adequate preparation. Teachers can begin to appreciate the value of multiethnic education when they become familiar with the concept. Unfortunately, most educators have received their entire professional training from institutions devoid of training in ethnic and cultural diversity. The lack of teacher preparation in this area, either pre-service or in-service, is more often than not the case. This situation has created a teacher population less knowledgeable about teaching ethnic content than it might otherwise be. As long as this state of affairs exists, the burden and/or responsibility for training teachers in multiethnic education falls primarily upon in-service programs. In addition, individual teachers may also find it necessary to assume some responsibility for their own instruction in this area.

Recent efforts of the National Council for the Accreditation of Teacher Education (NCATE) in revising the Standards for Accreditation to include training for future teachers in multicultural education should contribute greatly to filling this void. Other encouraging signs are the work of the Teacher Corps in enhancing in-service education, and the possibilities of teacher centers for helping to fill this gap cannot go unnoticed.

Because the absence of training in this area implies a possible lack of interest in and sensitivity to the necessity and value of multiethnic education, unless the individual school and/or school district has provisions for encouraging teacher participation in multiethnic in-service training, these programs may not have total involvement. This same premise may hold true for individual teachers who may be reticent about developing individualized programs of instruction. In order to encourage the involvement and participation of teachers, some effort will need to be exerted to convince them of their importance in the successful implementation of the program, including an awareness of the value of multiethnic education to both student and teacher.

For the minority student the multiethnic approach can serve to enhance the worth of self. Strong self-concepts tend to serve as motivating forces and can encourage academic achievement, and minority students need to know that they are a legitimate part of this society. The nonminority student can gain a more realistic view of the world and an exposure to cultural differences that can lead to a better understanding of self in relation to others. The nonminority child also needs to know of the contributions that other people have made to build this nation.

35

As for the teacher, I can still feel the joy, the excitement, and the sense of accomplishment from my first experience with multiethnic instruction. There is something very special about providing learning experiences to students that expose them to ethnic and cultural diversity. If carefully executed, such exposure can open avenues for exploration and learning that can only add richness to the education of those involved.

PREPARING TO TEACH MULTIETHNIC EDUCATION

When I first thought about including ethnic content in the curriculum of my fourth grade classroom, I was overwhelmed by the thought of becoming sufficiently prepared to do an effective job. There seemed to be so much I needed to know and I wasn't quite sure how or where to start. I was comfortable only with the fact that I wanted to become involved, and I was beginning to realize how unfair it was to deny students opportunities to learn about ethnic and cultural diversity. It took me a while, however, to organize my thoughts and to think through the necessary steps to prepare myself.

A First Step

Then I realized that I had already made the initial step in becoming prepared; I was motivated! I realized that as an educator I had certain responsibilities. I felt that education is a process in a democratic society that can excite students with the possibility of a full life. This possibility is limited only by the knowledge, curiosity, and imagination of the student. My responsibility was to help students broaden their expectations and live fuller lives. In fulfilling this responsibility I had to help students understand the pressures in society that lead to isolation and prejudice. I also had to help them discover ways to create a society that can be free of ethnic and racial biases.[8] Unfortunately, very little is being done to counter the biased and prejudiced attitudes that develop among American students. Students are rarely exposed to accurate information about racial differences. This failure limits students' understanding of others and such silence can lead to the perpetuation of existing myths about people that are prevalent in the larger society. I realized that the task of counteracting racial biases was difficult but essential for the maintenance and continued development of a democratic society.[9] In spite of the difficulty, I knew that I wanted to approach this task by accepting the responsibility for teaching a multiethnic curriculum.

Gaining Content

Although motivation was important, I knew that I needed much more. My second step was to learn more about the ethnic cultures I wanted to introduce to my students, particularly the history and the involvement of specific groups of people in the development of this country. Before I could incorporate this information into the curriculum, many questions needed answers. For a time it seemed an overwhelming project. How would I find the time to do the required research and continue to develop lesson plans and gather material for current classroom activities? Looking for the most convenient way to acquire the necessary content, I divided the information into two types: one dealing with diversity in general, to provide a broad understanding of ethnicity and culture; the other focusing more specifically on individual ethnic and cultural groups. Much of the reading, preparation, and time that I was already spending on teaching could be reorganized and redirected to help me accomplish my goal.

One very important decision at the outset was to limit my first attempt by focusing on one ethnic group. This approach allowed greater concentration on certain aspects. It also helped me acquire the information needed to begin to teach. Later, I could add another ethnic group to my course of study and I could continue in this manner indefinitely. I was ready to begin! A quick survey of all the things I did to remain intellectually alert as well as to prepare for my responsibility in the classroom produced the following activities: I read newspapers, periodicals, novels, and children's books; I attended movies; I visited museums; I previewed movies and filmstrips for classroom use; and I occasionally attended lectures or events at a nearby university where I also took several courses once or twice a year. Not only was I doing much more than I was aware of, but in every instance I recognized that the focus for each activity could be structured so that the subject of the reading, the museums visits, the film and filmstrip previewing, as well as the courses, could be on the ethnic group under consideration. I was using the same amount of time, continuing with my usual classroom preparation, but at the same time gaining the content needed to teach a multiethnic curriculum. A task that at first glance appeared to be overwhelming was suddenly reduced to one that was now manageable and provided some challenge, as well as fun and information.

Preparing to teach a multiethnic curriculum requires motivation, the desire to teach ethnic content. Teaching ethnic content demands that the teacher have a firm grasp on certain kinds of information necessary for adequate presentation of facts. And in order to provide effective multiethnic instruction some attention must be given to the manner in which the instruction is imparted to the student, the "how" of presenting the material. My attention soon turned to the implementation aspects of a multiethnic curriculum.

Teaching Methods and Strategies

Most of my teaching involved presenting information in the form of units of study. I found this method effective because it allowed me to organize an abbreviated course of study in the subject areas for which I was responsible. Because this approach is an interesting way to present material, I thought it might also prove to be effective in teaching ethnic content. After learning more about ethnic and cultural diversity, however, I acquired a better understanding of the rationale for teaching ethnic content and decided the unit approach was not the best one to use. In my opinion, presenting information about an ethnic group in a single unit style tends to separate the contributions and the involvement of the group from the total historical picture of this country. The unit method has value, however, in situations where emphasis and concentrated study are important. But to expose young children to ethnic content in this manner can encourage a separatist view, which is not a goal of multiethnic instruction. Such content is far more valuable if it is integrated throughout the curriculum and presented where appropriate. The fact that most of what children learn about ethnic and racial biases is taught to them in a subtle way further convinced me that the reverse can be taught in the same manner.

I initiated my efforts by selecting only one subject area for concentration, after learning a great deal about the ethnic group chosen for study for the first six months of that year and feeling comfortable with my progress. Reading was the subject area I selected for exposing my fourth graders to information on Black Americans. Integrating the material into the reading activities of the class became an exciting venture. During listening time I read an autobiography of a Black American to the class. I made sure that the classroom library collection contained several books about Blacks from which students could choose. I prepared listening tapes of interesting stories involving Black characters and/or containing some relevant material. I selected filmstrips for the reading corner, which also contained information on Blacks. I made sure that all the reading activities were integrated with material about Blacks; but, even more importantly, I made sure that the information presented was timely, meaningful, and appropriate. For example, I introduced the class to Crispus Attucks when the reading text presented stories about the American Revolution. We discussed the involvement of Blacks in the events of that period and the impact of these events on the historical development of the country. The material presented was supplemental to what appeared in the reading series; it was appropriate and timely! An effort to correlate writing experiences with reading activity encouraged me to develop a unit on poetry which then allowed the introduction of Phillis Wheatley. The study of her life gave the class an opportunity to better understand some of the implications of slavery. The poetry unit also paved the way for other creative writing experiences that included a comparison of myths and fables. At this point it was quite appropriate to include stories about West African countries, which led to some work in geography and an opportunity to explore the African heritage of Black Americans.

My first attempt could not have been so successful if I had not acquired the necessary background information. *Establishing a knowledge base* was an extremely important factor. Although I began the entire process after developing a rationale for teaching ethnic content, the more involved I became, the more clearly I could see that I had *developed a philosophy* for teaching a multiethnic curriculum. Once I had *established a knowledge base* and *developed a philosophy,* I was ready to teach, and *implementation* was a pleasure.

The following semester I branched out, beginning to focus on another ethnic group. The second attempt was easier because I knew where to go for the information I needed and I was encouraged by the success of my earlier efforts. Two factors determined my success: (1) the attitudes and behavior I observed in my students and (2) the way I felt about my new teaching approach. The students were excited about what they were learning and they were becoming involved—asking questions, bringing materials from home, reading the books I had placed in the classroom, and beginning to see relationships between current events and information discussed in class. Their enthusiasm about learning was encouraging and served to nurture my sense of motivation.

As I continued to discover relevant information for teaching, I became much more aware of the value of using an integrated approach to multiethnic education. Opportunities for correlating and coordinating ethnic content were many and varied, the most convenient area being social studies. A unit on safety, for example, was appropriate for including information about the contributions of Garrett Morgan and it provided the basis for moving into the study of transportation. A unit on transportation offered an excellent opportunity to bring Harriet Tubman to the attention of the class when, after studying the most traditional modes of transportation, it was most appropriate for the class to examine the meaning of the "underground railway." Art presented an interesting opportunity for delving into the cultures of several ethnic groups; several exciting periods developed from a comparison of masks from a variety of ethnic groups and cultures. The students' creations took on a different meaning once they had an understanding of the relationship of masks to the respective groups.

With an increasing sensitivity to the selection and development of instructional materials, I no longer used any material merely because it was available but evaluated it to ensure that it contained objective information about ethnic and cultural groups. My guidelines for evaluation were informal. I scrutinized textbooks as well as tradebooks, examining the written material as thoroughly as I did the pictorial content. I looked for materials that were not biased, that were accurate and objective in presenting facts. I searched for hidden messages in pictorial representations—what were the pictures teaching? More often than not, I discovered materials that should not be used or that, if used, required a careful and sensitive approach. The absence of appropriate commercially prepared materials for multiethnic instruction was an encouragement to develop materials for classroom use.

By the end of the second semester of teaching a multiethnic curriculum, I was able to assess my progress and could clearly identify the stages. The first stage of implementation—*initiating*—was very successful. I found a place to begin and selected the area of reading as the starting point. Once I felt comfortable with the initial efforts, I moved to the second stage and began *integrating*. It was quite easy to incorporate ethnic content into science and social studies once I had gained the necessary information, which I made very sure was timely, meaningful, and appropriate. Then, I was ready to move ahead into the final stage —*enriching*. Plans for enriching were never-ending for I could already tell that there is no possible way to exhaust all there is to learn about the different contributions made by various ethnic groups. I was also able to enhance my teaching by integrating ethnic content into the other subject areas of the curriculum. While information and content were valuable, there was, in addition, a challenge in creating and developing teaching methods and strategies that would help accomplish the task.

CONCLUSION

My experiences confirmed that the success of multiethnic education does depend largely on the teacher. The students in my classroom demonstrated that the negative attitudes of children about people who differ from them can be influenced by the teacher. It was evident, that as a teacher, I played a significant role in affecting change in their behavior as well. I also discovered that certain of my own predispositions about differences among and between people were influenced by my exposure to accurate and objective information about various ethnic and cultural groups. And I was constantly reminded of the importance of support from the principal, who encouraged my efforts in a great many ways. It was also helpful to know that although the district had not adopted a policy, it was forthcoming.

Organizing for the teaching of a multiethnic curriculum can be challenging and not too difficult if the preparation begins with *establishing a knowledge base* to encourage the *development of a philosophy,* which provides the supporting rationale for becoming involved in the *implementation* of a multiethnic curriculum. Teaching a multiethnic curriculum can be made easier if the first efforts of *initiating* are small and manageable. Once success is obvious, then more extensive attempts can be made toward *integrating* content into a greater portion of the curriculum. When these two stages are accomplished, the final stage of *enriching* can provide the climate so vital for successful implementation of multiethnic education.

REFERENCES

1. Wilbur B. Brookover and Edsel L. Erickson, *Society, Schools and Learning* (Boston: Allyn and Bacon, 1969).

2. Kenneth B. Clark, *Prejudice and Your Child* (Boston: Beacon Press, 1955).

3. Mary Ellen Goodman, *Race Awareness in Young Children* (London: Collier-Macmillan, 1952).

4. Bruno Lasker, *Racial Attitudes in Children* (New York: New American Library, 1970).

5. William W. Joyce and James A. Banks, eds., *Teaching the Language Arts to Culturally Different Children* (Reading, Mass.: Addison-Wesley, 1971), p. 262.

6. Maxine Dunfee, *Ethnic Modification of the Curriculum* (Washington, D.C.: Association for Supervision and Curriculum Development, 1969).

7. Gertrude Noar, *Sensitizing Teachers to Ethnic Groups* (New York: Anti-Defamation League of B'nai B'rith, 1971), p. 2.

8. Charlotte Epstein, *Intergroup Relations for the Classroom Teacher* (Boston: Houghton Mifflin Co., 1968), p. 58.

9. J. Kenneth Morland, "The Development of Racial Bias in Young Children," in *Teaching Social Studies to Culturally Different Children,* eds. James A. Banks and William W. Joyce (Reading, Mass.: Addison-Wesley, 1971), p. 31.

CHAPTER 4

Interactions in Culturally Pluralistic Classrooms

Geneva Gay

By far the greatest energy and efforts in multiethnic education to date have concentrated on explaining the concept, and developing curriculum guidelines for its implementation. In many ways, these emphases are expected, given the tendency to devote great amounts of time to materials production, ideological clarification, and sample curriculum designs early in the life of educational innovations.

Although important and necessary, these endeavors are not sufficient to adequately institutionalize the study of ethnic groups' histories, heritages, and cultures in all aspects of the American education system. Of equal importance to the future of multiethnic education in the 1980's is the need for increasing attention to evaluation practices, staff development, administrative policy and leadership, and the environmental context of the classroom in which multiethnic teaching and learning occur. This chapter focuses on interethnic group student-teacher interactions in culturally pluralistic classrooms. The basic premise underlying this focus is that the climate of culturally pluralistic classrooms is crucial to the success of multiethnic education since the "realities of the learning process . . . must be viewed in the context of the total arrangements and cultural practices that constitute education and the environment within which it operates."[1]

IMPORTANCE OF CLASSROOM CLIMATE TO INSTRUCTIONAL EFFECTIVENESS

A sizable body of literature exists, resulting from educational research, theory, and conventional wisdom about schooling, which supports the importance of classroom climate and interpersonal relations among students and teachers in determining the quality of instruction and student academic achievement. Most often these ideas have derived from research on teacher control of classroom instruction through patterns of verbal interactions with students (e.g., direct vs. indirect, authoritarian vs. democratic, divergent vs. convergent, open vs. closed), and the spatial/physical characteristics of the classroom itself (e.g., seating arrangements, temperature, lighting, decorum). The "hidden" curriculum, or values that instructional leaders teach by attitude and implicit example, is also considered an important "environmental factor" in the educational process. While these perceptions and characterizations of the classroom environment are important, we have chosen to focus here on some of the dimensions of interethnic group interactions among teachers and students in culturally pluralistic classrooms, the cultural conflicts that may occur, and the way in which these interactions and conflicts can negatively affect the teaching-learning process.

Several major premises undergird the arguments presented regarding the relationship between the climate (defined here as the interpersonal interactions among students and teachers from different ethnic and cultural backgrounds) of culturally pluralistic classrooms and the implementation of successful multiethnic education programs.

1. Cultural conflict is a critical factor in ethnically, socially, racially, and culturally pluralistic classrooms, which can significantly affect both the potential for and actual achievement of success or failure in teaching and learning.

2. Successful interpersonal relations among students and teachers in culturally and ethnically pluralistic school settings are requisite to the effective implementation of multiethnic education.

3. Teachers and other educational leaders should perceive culturally pluralistic classrooms as including different social systems, representing different ethnic groups. Each of these social systems has its own set of attitudes, values, beliefs, and behaviors.

4. Some degree of conflict among these different social systems is inevitable.

5. Many classroom behaviors exhibited by ethnically different students are culturally determined.

6. The best way to understand and improve interpersonal interactions among students and teachers in culturally pluralistic classrooms is through cultural analyses of classroom behaviors.

Teachers need to know what significant questions to ask about cultural differences among ethnic groups, how these differences are manifested in the classroom, how to find answers to questions of concern, and how to use resulting information to improve their interpersonal and instructional rapport with ethnically diverse students. Such cultural understandings are imperative in pluralistic classrooms because by the time ethnically different children

> begin their formal education . . . they have already internalized many of the basic values and beliefs of their native cultures, learned the rules of behavior which are considered appropriate for their role in the community, and established the procedures for continued socialization.[2]

For many ethnic students their culturally determined mind sets about teaching and learning are incompatible with the normative expectations of schools. A major challenge to classroom teachers of these students is to minimize, if not resolve, the points of incompatibility between school and ethnic orientations toward learning in order to maximize the academic payoff potential of their instructional efforts.

INEVITABILITY OF CLASSROOM CONFLICT

Anticipations of conflict and controversy with students from different ethnic backgrounds is often a source of anxiety for individuals considering teaching in culturally and ethnically pluralistic schools. This anxiety can be minimized if teachers understand and accept two basic factors about human interactions, especially in culturally pluralistic settings. First, there is no way that *all* conflict can be avoided in any classroom, whether it is culturally, ethnically, or socially homogeneous or heterogeneous. The key question, then, is not how to eliminate conflict, but how to minimize it and constructively channel it toward instructional purposes. Second, with sufficient knowledge about cultural differences and adequate observation skills, *points of potential conflict* among different ethnic group norms and cultural lifestyles are identifiable. And, if they are identifiable they can be managed, often avoided, and/or redirected to facilitate rather than to inhibit teaching and learning.

Classroom conflict results when individuals and groups with different goals, values, attitudes, and behavioral patterns attempt to live and work together in somewhat constricted spatial limitations, as is the case in most school situations. The potential for conflict to materialize increases considerably when students and teachers do not share similar ethnic identities, cultural codes, value systems, and background experiences.

Three types of conflict are most common in pluralistic classrooms and other settings where different social systems exist side by side.

1. *Procedural* conflicts involve disagreements over courses of action to be taken to reach some stated goal.

2. *Substantive* conflicts stem from incompatible goals. For example, the academic goals and expectations of teachers are often at odds with the social and personal goals of their ethnic students.

3. *Interpersonal* conflicts exist when different sets of attitudes, beliefs, and values are held by different groups and individuals.[3] A case in point is the conflict between the "home cultures" of the ethnic groups and the culture of the school.

All these types of conflict operate in culturally pluralistic classrooms, but the latter are the most consequential for multiethnic education.

Major interpersonal conflicts occur in culturally pluralistic classrooms for those students whose ethnic identities and cultural backgrounds differ significantly from the mainstream norms of the school. Such students frequently experience "psychological transitional traumas" as they try to determine when and how to move back and forth between the expectations of the school and of their "home" cultures. Such transitions require mental, emotional, and psychological energies that could otherwise be directed toward academic tasks. When these transitions are not accomplished easily, they can cause students much anxiety and frustration. These frustrations, in turn, may be expressed as hostility toward teachers and other students, disinterest in classroom activities, or withdrawal from any kind of classroom interactions.

When students from different ethnic backgrounds find themselves in these intrapsychic conflict situations, they may choose to meet either individual or institutional needs. If they choose to meet institutional needs (to conform to school and classroom norms and expectations), they are likely to experience unsatisfactory *personal integration* in the classroom, and to become frustrated and confused about themselves. If they choose to satisfy individual or ethnic needs (to practice "home" cultural values, beliefs, behaviors), they are liable to unsatisfactory *role adjustment* in the classroom, and to be ineffective as students.[4] Undoubtedly, this is the kind of dilemma many ethnically different students encounter in pluralistic classrooms. The higher the degree of their personal sense of ethnic identity, ethnic group association, and cultural consciousness, the greater the prospect of their experiencing cultural conflict in the classroom. This is especially so if their ethnicity and culture are not sanctioned by school norms, that is, Anglo-centric and middle class. The probability for conflict is great because ethnically diverse students and teachers are frequently "prepared for quite different patterns of activity through different modes of training and experience, through orientation to different systems of value, motivation toward different goals, and through the creation of different needs."[5]

In some situations ethnic students in culturally pluralistic classrooms are caught in double-edged conflicts. Their personal need-dispositions are different from the institutional expectations of both the classroom culture *and* their respective native cultures. Consider, for example, the case of the Mexican-American students who are labeled "gringos" and "tacos" by other Mexican-Americans because they are not being "ethnic enough," and rejected by Anglo students and teachers because their "Mexican-Americanness" is not valued. Or the Black students who are seen as "Afro-Saxons," "oreos," or "toms" by other Blacks, yet who find it difficult to relate and adjust successfully to school norms and expectations. Or the Italian-American students who are "wops" to other Italian-Americans as well as to Anglos. In effect, these students are "marginal individuals"; they are accepted neither by their ethnic groups nor by the school culture. Such a state of existence is not conducive to either personal psychological well-being or productive academic performance. Situations like these present a critical challenge to teachers committed to multiethnic education—the challenge of how best to help these individuals resolve their ethnic dilemmas of self-identity, association with other members of their own ethnic group, and relating to ethnic others.

To understand why conflict situations exist in the classroom and how they can affect the instructional process, as well as to know how to develop ameliorating strategies, teachers need to examine the dynamics and various dimensions of cross-cultural interactions in pluralistic classrooms. They also need to become knowledgeable about those components of ethnic cultures which surface most frequently to challenge, overtly and subtly, school norms, values, and expectations. In other words, teachers need to become more consciously aware of and sensitive to the ways in which the cultural conditioning of ethnic students within their own ethnic communities differs from school socialization patterns.

The resulting insights can be an invaluable aid in making more viable decisions concerning methods for increasing the success of schooling for ethnically and culturally different students.

DIMENSIONS OF CULTURAL PLURALISM IN CLASSROOMS

In order to understand the interpersonal relations among students and teachers in culturally pluralistic classrooms, and their effect on the instructional process, many different cultural factors should be examined. Of particular importance to teachers and other school personnel are those ethnic beliefs, attitudes, and behaviors associated with learning styles, relational patterns, value systems, and communication habits. These are the areas which seem to cause the greatest conflict and dissension among students and teachers from different ethnic and cultural backgrounds.

It is impossible to discuss any one or all of these factors in great detail here. Some illustrative examples in only two of them—patterns of teaching and learning, and communication—are presented to demonstrate the kinds of questions to ask, the points of departure, and the priority emphases to employ in the systematic study of interethnic group interactions in culturally pluralistic classrooms. The knowledge and insights deriving from such studies are fundamental to changing the classroom atmosphere or climate so that it complements formal instructional efforts and activities to implement effective multiethnic educational programs.

Ethnic Learning Patterns, Cultural Values, and Classroom Teaching

A growing body of research and theoretical literature is emerging on the interrelationship between ethnic learning styles, cultural values, and interpersonal relations, and their effects on student and teacher behaviors in the classroom. Some agreement exists among several researchers on the primary characteristics of two major categories of learning styles, the analtyical or field-independent and the relational or field-sensitive.[6] Some significant discrepancies have also been found to exist between the most predominant teaching style of the public schools ("analytical") and the learning style of many ethnic groups ("relational").

Studies of ethnic group cultures in the United States indicate that learning style preferences or inclinations are closely associated with family structures, child-rearing practices, and cultural patterns of interpersonal relations. For example, individuals socialized in cultural communities which prioritize group achievement, cooperation, obedience and deference to authority, and "persons over objects" tend to be externally motivated, dependent upon praise and reinforcement from significant others, and more readily responsive to human-interest, socially oriented curriculum content in learning situations. Comparatively, ethnic communities which emphasize individualism, assertiveness, personal initiative, and material well-being in socializing their young are likely to produce students who are more analytical, competitive, impersonal, individualistic, and task-oriented in their learning behaviors. These latter learning patterns tend to be more compatible with the prevailing teaching styles found in most public schools.

In examining learning and teaching styles, and analyzing their implications for creating better culturally pluralistic classroom climates, educators should remember that *individual* dimensions and manifestations of learning and teaching behaviors exist within established cultural or ethnic group patterns. Furthermore, descriptions of ethnic learning patterns and teaching styles represent *cultural configurations for groups, not specific behaviors of any given individual within the group.* In other words, "ethnic propensities, inclinations, tendencies, and specific characteristics persist within large population groups but not necessarily in specific individuals."[7] Therefore, while it may indeed be true that the most dominant instructional style practiced in American public schools is "analytical and impersonal," all teachers will *not* operate this way. Similarly, while the learning style that seems most characteristic of many Appalachian Whites and Hispanics is highly relational, cooperative, and person-oriented, there will be some individual students from each of these ethnic groups who will not exhibit any of the characteristics ascribed to their respective ethnic group. Others will exhibit some of the learning style characteristics in varying degrees and/or circumstances. The same is true for Anglo-Americans. As a group, their learning pattern is primarily analytical (and thus quite compatible with the patterns approved by schools), but, as individuals, many variations exist among them.

Obviously, then, allowances must be made for individual differences in any considerations of ethnic and cultural group learning styles. But teachers should not use these allowances to attempt to invalidate the existence of ethnic *group* learning styles. As Stodolsky and Lesser explain, social class, experience, and intellect can cause individual variations within ethnic group learning styles by affecting the *level* of personal academic performance. However, *group patterns* of cognitive processing (e.g., learning style) are ethnically and culturally determined, and *"once the pattern specific to the ethnic group emerges, social class variations within the group do not alter this basic organization."*[8]

Discrepancies between classroom teaching styles and ethnic group learning styles can cause severe conflict in culturally pluralistic school settings, and can create an environment wherein successful teaching and learning are virtually impossible. Rosalie Cohen suggests that

> so discrepant are the analytic and relational frames of reference that a pupil whose preferred mode of cognitive organization is empathically relational is unlikely to be rewarded in the school setting either socially or by grades, regardless of his native abilities and even if his information repertoire and background of experience is adequate.[9]

If this is true, the effective implementation of multiethnic education is as much a function of the compatibility of teaching styles and different ethnic group learning styles as it is of developing creative curriculum designs and employing imaginative instructional strategies in studying ethnic group heritages, cultures, and experiences.

Communication Behaviors

Three points about communication make it a significant factor to consider in analyzing the classroom climate and student-teacher interactions in ethnically and culturally pluralistic schools.

1. Effective communication is the single most important requirement for effective teaching.

2. "The communication behavior of a teacher or a student is largely the result of the social system and culture the individual grew up in."[10]

3. Communication is an area of human relations that is very susceptible to misunderstanding, especially in cross-cultural and/or interethnic group interactions.

An understanding of the full impact of different ethnic and cultural communication styles on interpersonal relations and instructional processes requires more than a linguistic analysis. Teachers should also be aware of the cultural messages embedded in language structures and communication habits of various ethnic groups. For example, knowledge of the linguistic structure of Spanish may help teachers understand the vocabulary and syntax of the language Spanish-speaking students use in the classroom. But, without a *cultural understanding* of some other dimensions of Hispanic culture and communication behaviors, teachers are likely *not* to comprehend some significant *messages* students are sending. A knowledge of the structure and form of Cantonese can be useful to teachers of students who speak this language, but it alone will not enable them to understand why Chinese-American students from traditional family backgrounds tend to be verbally passive in the classroom and prefer mechanical instructional tasks over verbal and expressive tasks. Thus, teachers must understand that ethnic group communication styles are both linguistic systems and expressions of cultural systems.

Without an understanding of their cultural foundations, neither the communication habits of ethnic groups nor their potential effects on the teaching-learning process can be fully comprehended. For instance, the emphasis on a written and cognitive communication style in most American schools reflects certain rules of form, order, structure, and direction which derive largely from Anglo-centric values of rationality, object-centeredness, and passive-receptive relations between speakers and audiences. An understanding of the communication habits of some Black Americans in classrooms is facilitated by knowledge and awareness of such cultural information as (1) the emphasis given to developing verbal dexterity within Black socialization processes; (2) the perception and use of words as power devices; (3) the fact that Black culture stems from an oral tradition; (4) the significance of style and delivery in communication among Black Americans; and (5) the important role of nonverbal nuances, symbolism, and metaphoric language in Black communication. To respond appropriately to the verbal passivity of many Native American and Chinese-American students, teachers need to understand that they are socialized in their families and ethnic communities more toward visual learning through observation and imitation than toward verbal activity. To learn how to adjust classroom climates, student-teacher interactions, and learning activities to accommodate the "cultural proclivity" of Italian-Americans, Hispanics, and Blacks to be more metaphoric and kinesically expressive than objectively descriptive in their communication behaviors, teachers must know something about the ethnic heritages, the cultural conditioning, the lifestyles, and the values systems of these groups, as well as how and when these behaviors are manifested in the classroom.

Richard Porter suggests that teachers should be familiar with seven critical communication factors beyond linguistic structural characteristics: attitudes, social organization, patterns of thought, role prescriptions, use and organization of space, time, and nonverbal nuances.[11] Hurt, Scott, and McCroskey also suggest giving greater attention to nonverbal factors in cross-cultural communication. Among the list of nonverbal communication components they recommend for analysis are proxemics, touch, body movements, gestures, differentiations in response-time patterns, use and quality of voice, eye behavior, and usage of objects.[12]

Nonverbal communication messages are crucial in creating a constructive environment to facilitate productive teaching and learning in pluralistic classrooms. As Hurt, Scott, and McCroskey explain:

> Most people, including students, believe that our nonverbal communication is under less conscious control than our verbal. Thus, our nonverbal messages are seen as more honest reflections of what we are *really* thinking or feeling at a particular time. Many of the cues students use to make judgments about a teacher's competence or character are obtained by observing the teacher's nonverbal behavior.[13]

These observations are true about nonverbal communication in general; they are particularly true in culturally pluralistic classroom settings.

Many nonverbal communication behaviors in pluralistic classrooms are culturally determined. Failure to understand this, and the source, can result in serious cultural conflicts. For example, the timing of a student's response to a teacher's directive may be perceived as inattentiveness or inability if it is slow in coming, or impetuosity and academic sloppiness if it is too fast. Teachers may encourage those students who respond slowly (even though their cultural inclination is to use a slow pace in talking) to "not take so long in getting your thoughts together," for "we can't wait all day on you," or "you are impeding the progress of the entire class." Or they may admonish those students who respond quickly to "think about your answers before responding" and to "slow down." The implicit assumptions are that the students cannot think—and do it well—as rapidly as they seem to be doing, and that talking at a fast pace is somehow undesirable. In some cultural and ethnic groups body movements and gestures are used liberally as the level, intensity, and emotional involvement in communication acts increase. These nonverbal nuances also play a major role in determining the effectiveness of the communication *messages* being delivered. Other ethnic individuals, however, may consider such "gyrations" as distractions which interfere with the effectiveness of the person's intended message. Some students are perceived negatively, criticized, and even penalized in instruction if they speak too softly, in a high pitch, in dialect, and/or with an accent. Whereas in one culture direct eye contact is a necessary condition to signal "attending behavior," in another it may be considered a sign of disrespect and defiance. The practice of "eye aversion" has been found to exist among Blacks, Hispanics, and Native Americans. The role prescription of listeners in one culture as motivators and stimulators of a speaker's level and quality of performance may be perceived as instigation of troublemaking, disturbance, rudeness, and classroom management problems for teachers from a different ethnic and cultural background. A case in point is that of Black American patterns of listening and responding to speakers. If Black listeners find the comments of a speaker (teacher, minister, performer) engaging, stimulating, provocative, or otherwise personally pleasing, they are likely to "talk back" to the speaker. This "talking back" takes the form of audio, vocal, and/or motor responses, which serve as motivation for the speaker to "rap on." Teachers frequently interpret these "normal Black cultural patterns of listener responding behaviors" as noise, discourtesy, inattentiveness, rudeness, and disrespect.

The conceivable points of cultural clash in the area of communication in pluralistic classrooms are numerous. The intent here has not been to list all of them. Rather, it has been (1) to suggest the magnitude and significance of these sources of cultural differences for creating a classroom environment conducive to or destructive of instructional effectiveness; (2) to argue that many of them are culturally determined, and can be best understood through cultural analysis; and (3) to explain the role they can and should play in improving interpersonal relations among students and teachers from different ethnic backgrounds in culturally pluralistic classrooms, and ultimately, in the implementation of quality multiethnic education in schools.

CONCLUSION

Before multiethnic education is successfully institutionalized in all dimensions of the American educational enterprise, much remains to be done. Its future will depend as much on the attitudinal frames of reference of instructional leaders toward ethnic diversity and cultural pluralism, and the environmental contexts in which it takes place, as it will on the quality of the curriculum designs, materials, and instructional strategies employed.

Interethnic group relations and interactions among students and teachers in culturally pluralistic classrooms create a powerful environmental context for the success or failure of multiethnic educational activities in the formal structure of teaching and learning. Unless educators attend to the cultural factors—learning styles, value systems, relational patterns, and communication habits—which determine the environmental sets or climates of culturally pluralistic classrooms, other attempts to implement multiethnic education are likely to be minimized. In assessing the potential and promise for the future of multiethnic education in American schools, it is therefore imperative that educators give as much attention and consideration to the informal and interpersonal climate of culturally pluralistic classrooms as to the formal instructional processes.

REFERENCES

1. S. T. Kimball, *Culture and the Educative Process: Anthropological Perperspective* (New York: Teachers College Press, 1974), p. 78.

2. M. Saville-Troike, *A Guide to Culture in the Classroom* (Rosslyn, Va.: National Clearinghouse for Bilingual Education, 1978), p. 7.

3. H. T. Hurt, M. D. Scott, and J. C. McCroskey, *Communication in the Classroom* (Reading, Mass.: Addison-Wesley Publishing Co.), 1978.

4. Ibid., p. 74.

5. A. I. Hallowell, "Cultural Factors in the Structuralization of Perception," in *Intercultural Communication: A Reader,* eds. L. A. Samovar and R. E. Porter (Belmont, Calif.: Wadsworth Publishing Co., 1972), p. 50.

6. For details on ethnic learning styles, see M. Ramírez and A. Castañeda, *Cultural Democracy, Bicognitive Development, and Education* (New York: Academic Press, 1974); M. Ramírez and D. R. Price-Williams, "Cognitive Styles of Children of Three Ethnic Groups in the United States," *Journal of Cross-Cultural Psychology* 3, no. 1 (June 1974): 212–19; A. Castañeda and T. Gray, "Bicognitive Processes in Multicultural Education," *Educational Leadership* 32, no. 3 (December 1974): 203–07; R. A. Cohen, "Conceptual Styles, Cultural Conflict, and Nonverbal Tests of Intelligence," in *Schooling in the Cultural Context,* eds. J. I. Roberts and S. K. Akinsanya (New York: David McKay Co., 1976), pp. 290–332; and L. Morris, ed., *Extracting Learning Styles from Social/Cultural Diversity: Studies of Five American Minorities* (Southwest Teacher Corps Network, 1978).

7. A. M. Greeley, "Too Much Ado About Ethnicity? Church Should Rejoice in It," *Momentum* 6, no. 3 (October 1975): 19.

8. S. S. Stodolsky and G. Lesser, "Learning Patterns in the Disadvantaged," *Harvard Educational Review* 67 (1967): 567.

9. Cohen, "Conceptual Styles," p. 292.

10. Hurt, Scott, and McCroskey, *Communication in the Classroom,* p. 22.

11. R. E. Porter, "An Overview of Intercultural Communication," in *Intercultural Communication: A Reader,* eds. L. A. Samovar and R. E. Porter (Belmont, Calif.: Wadsworth Publishing Co, 1972), pp. 3–18.

12. Hurt, Scott, and McCroskey, *Communication in the Classroom.*

13. Ibid., p. 92.

CHAPTER 5

The School Culture
and the Cultures of Minority Students

Tomás A. Arciniega

Improving the response of public education to ethnic minority youngsters is the most important challenge facing the schools of this country in the decade ahead. Given the deteriorating condition of urban environments, schools have no choice but to play a larger and larger role in the lives of children from low-income backgrounds, most of whom are members of ethnic minorities.

The challenge is clear: we must develop better approaches. The development of more viable school programs must begin, however, with a recognition, especially by teachers and principals, of the functionality of ethnic minority lifestyles for coping with societal realities. The programming and day-to-day actions of the entire school staff should demonstrate that ethnic affiliation and identification with group behaviors among inner-city youngsters are considered positive coping behaviors to be fostered as a source of individual strength. Educational activities should communicate clearly in form and practice that our schools really value the intrinsic worth of every child, striving also to reach beyond the mere awareness of obvious ethnic differences.

Effecting meaningful changes in the schools' response to ethnic minorities requires the communication of a positive and overt affirmation of the "rightness and worth" of ethnic and cultural differences in children. Such a view embraces the value premise that the promotion of cultural pluralism and cultural alternatives is something so basic and important to America that it must be made an integral part of the educational experience of every one of our youngsters. In its classic statement on multicultural education, the American Association of Colleges for Teacher Education underscores the importance of this point:

> To endorse cultural pluralism is to endorse the principle that there is no one model American. To endorse cultural pluralism is to understand and appreciate the differences that exist among the nation's citizens. It is to see these differences as a positive force in the continuing development of a society which professes a wholesome respect for the intrinsic worth of every individual. Cultural pluralism is more than a temporary accommodation to placate racial and ethnic minorities. It is a concept that aims toward a heightened sense of being and of wholeness of the entire society based on the unique strengths of each of its parts.[1]

Despite the millions of federal dollars invested in programs aimed at improving the educational lot of Blacks and other minorities during the past fifteen years, progress has been painfully slow. As Richard DeLone points out in his controversial book *Small Futures,* recent U.S. efforts to close the gap between the upper and lower socioeconomic classes through educational and other social interventions have in fact had little impact. Schools and other major institutional activities continue to be geared to serve primarily the needs of the White nonpoor, resulting in the virtual exclusion of the economically disadvantaged from the intended benefits of all major social service programs.[2]

Reversing that trend will not be easy. In order to change the status quo, three kinds of action commitments are necessary.

1. Schools need to recognize the existence of the problem and accept it as "their problem."

2. Schools will need to commit themselves to working collaboratively to find ways and means to develop workable solutions to "their problem."

3. Teachers and principals must accept the need to take the long view. Time and patience are essential qualities for would-be reformers.

RECOGNIZING THE EXISTENCE AND THE NATURE OF "THE PROBLEM"

The organizational problem of how to change schools to more adequately meet the needs of ethnic minority students is a complex one.

It is tremendously complex primarily because educational systems quite accurately reflect the existent socioeconomic stratification and makeup of the communities they serve. The goals of school organizations and the ways in which they are operationalized depend upon the allocation process of the particular regional system. Organizational territories in all communities clearly indicate what, who, how, and to what extent the society values the various goals it assigns. In other words, organizational terrains can tell us what and who are considered important and for what purpose. Thus the problem of changing schools to better meet the needs of ethnic minority students is one aspect of the more encompassing issue: how to change through social action programs certain key interrelated structural practices in any given community system.

Meaningful changes require authentic involvement on a total system basis in what is "really going on" in schools. The task of analyzing the organizational response of schools, as they seek to provide more relevant education for minority youngsters, is impossible to separate from the more global response of the community as a whole to the problem of providing more authentic access for ethnic minority students to the mainstream of American life.

In responding to pressures for change in meeting minority student needs, too many school systems have used hold-the-line, resistive strategies. They have consistently opposed making major alterations in traditional goals. Typically their response to the challenge of a better education for minorities is characterized by increased efforts to socialize and influence incumbents in the system to accept traditional approaches. This may be accomplished in a variety of ways: outright coercion, through the system of extrinsic incentives and rewards; increased emphasis on adherence to existing rules and regulations; status-promotion allocations, co-option, and other measures.

In addition, resistive school systems also promote the status quo by increased efforts to "properly" socialize the clients of the system and their parents. These groups must also be convinced of the appropriateness of the system's response lest they, too, mount serious pressures to change school organizational goals. Incumbents, clients, and their parents are thus recipients of systematic persuasive efforts to convince them that major changes in the prevailing state of things are not good for the organization—*not good for them!*

It is a fact that our school systems have not been as successful with ethnic minority and lower socioeconomic status (SES) White youngsters as they have been with middle- and upper-class White students. Traditional responses to educating the culturally and ethnically different have not been more successful because the school systems have reacted to this challenge in overly traditional ways. For the most part they have simply labored to expand and improve past practices. In other words, *with minor modifications they have continued doing what has not worked before!* Lack of success has then been attributed to limited resources or the federal government.

As Banks[3] and others have consistently pointed out, the failure of traditional approaches stems from the false assumption that the problem lies primarily *within a group.* Consequently, the school solutions are sought in the most effective ways to make over particular ethnic groups in the image of the middle-class majority. Whether the area to be changed is called their "value orientations," their "cultural or socioeconomic disadvantage," or more directly their "Mexicanness," or other ethnic label, the intent is clear: schools believe that society dictates the need to resocialize these youngsters along the lines of White middle-class values.

THE SPECIFICS OF CHANGE

Changing the organizational thrust must begin with an accurate identification of what needs to change. The major problem areas are five:

1. Pejorative and pathological perspective regarding the appropriateness, worth, and status of minority languages and dialects as bona fide media of instruction in the classroom

2. Inadequate treatment and presentation of the historical, cultural, and economic contributions made by ethnic minorities in the curricular programs of the schools

3. Underrepresentation of ethnic minorities in school district staffing patterns (teachers, administrators, counselors, etc.)

4. Lack of authentic involvement of minority communities in the decisionmaking structures of the school system

5. Testing, counseling, and guidance programs and processes based on a cultural deficit perspective of ethnic minority student needs.[4]

The search for viable solutions to these problems must begin with a commitment to change at the school site level. Teachers and principals are the key to successful reform. Their commitment to move on the issues involved is necessary. The process involved in working out how best to address the situation is probably more important than the specific strategies ultimately developed and agreed upon.

Whatever the specifics, the planned reforms should clearly delineate the direction for change. The five problem areas identified can be rephrased in terms of goals for that purpose as follows:

Goal 1: Recognition of the appropriateness, worth, and status of minority languages and dialects as bona fide media of instruction in the classroom

Goal 2: Adequate treatment and presentation in the curriculum of the historical, cultural, and economic contributions made by minorities to American society

Goal 3: Adequate representation of ethnic minorities in school district staffing patterns (teachers, administrators, counselors, etc.)

Goal 4: Full and representative participation by the minority communities in the decisionmaking structures of the school system

Goal 5: Development of a testing, counseling, and guidance system based on a noncultural deficit perspective of ethnic minority student needs.[5]

The reform task facing each school then involves finding the best approach for *that* school for achieving each of the goals in context. Pushing together to achieve each goal is tremendously important. In some ways, creating the school climate to move in the right direction is more important than reaching the goals quickly.

The specifics for effecting the needed changes can be outlined rather easily. Doing something about them is, of course, another matter. The use of minority languages and dialects in the classroom, for example, is perhaps the most controversial issue. Much of the resistance to bilingual education stems from the erroneous belief that using the child's home language in teaching the curriculum of the school will somehow impede the learning of Standard English, despite ample research and data indicating rather unequivocally that, on the contrary, language minority youngsters in fact learn English faster and better in good bilingual programs.

The use of Black English is a somewhat parallel issue. Here the concern seems to stem from the fear that using the child's home dialect in any way in the school will somehow impede the learning of Standard English. The fears seem to be ill-founded since the intent in using the home dialect early and where appropriate is simply a method to better *reach* the child—to better enable the teacher to relate the school's program to the reality base of the child.

In both situations the mastering of Standard English is a basic goal. For bilingual children, however, the matter is more complicated since the mastery of the formal minority language is also included as a basic curricular goal. Trueba,[6] Lambert,[7] Ochoa and Rodriguez,[8] and other bilingual education specialists make a convincing case for sound bilingual instruction as a means for enabling *all* children to learn the state-mandated curriculum and become bilingual in the process.

Finding curricular materials which incorporate the contributions of ethnic minorities is an issue of paramount importance. Basic textbooks and classroom materials have not changed enough in the last ten years—despite the fact that this has been the most readily acknowledged problem in the compensatory education movement. Both teachers and principals need to search for materials which their students can relate to. This is certainly an area where teachers can have a major impact.

Achieving an adequate representation of minorities on the school staff is more than just an affirmative action issue. Ethnic minority children in inner-city schools need very much to feel that they and their kind belong in *their* school. There is no better and clearer way to communicate the school's recognition of this fact than through teachers, principals, and counselors they can identify with.

Likewise, the involvement of ethnic community members in the "real goings-on" of school decisionmaking is critically important. It is not easy to accomplish, but when minority parents and residents really develop a feeling of ownership for "their school," the difference is phenomenal. There are no sure-fire recipes for accomplishing this effectively, but it is clear that we have no choice. We have to try harder. Fortunately, the climate for achieving good and positive school-parent relationships has improved dramatically in the last few years.

The testing and counseling system issue is a particularly troublesome one. What is needed is a systemwide commitment to ensure that the test measures used by the district are culturally fair. Where the instruments used are not culturally fair, it is the district's responsibility to inform teachers and parents of the deficiencies. What is needed, above all, is a posture which communicates to ethnic minority youngsters in particular that the district, their schools, and their teachers have high expectations concerning their performance in school.

A related concern involves the need to keep a watchful eye on the ratio of ethnic minority youngsters in programs for the mentally retarded and the gifted, and in the noncollege vocational tracks. What about the dropout rate for particular ethnic categories? Are minority students making the honor rolls? All of these areas can be important indicators of progress and, conversely, important signals of problem situations.

CONCLUSION

As noted at the outset, there is no more important challenge facing those who work and direct schools than that of finding improved ways to meet the needs of ethnic minority and lower SES youngsters. Our major city school districts are now serving predominantly ethnic minority students. The impact of this new reality is only now beginning to make itself felt across levels of the educational establishment.

Public rejection of the civic obligation to adequately fund schools in the urban centers is not unrelated to this demographic shift. The serious downward trend in the economy has also served to spur the backlash that schools across the country have been experiencing.

Never before has public education been more in need of courageous and creative leadership. And never before has the importance of the roles of teacher and principal been more obvious. We need to recognize that fact and marshal the level and type of support required by school sites to meet the challenge. The 80's may well prove to be the decade of the swing back to a much-needed reemphasis on the individual school as the focus of attention and resources. I am hopeful that teachers and their principals, with help from the rest of us in the educational establishment, can rise to the occasion.

REFERENCES

1. AACTE's Commission on Multicultural Education, "No One Model American . . ." (Washington, D.C.: American Association of Colleges for Teacher Education, November 1973).

2. Richard H. DeLone and the Carnegie Council on Children, *Small Futures: Children, Inequality, and the Limits of Liberal Reform* (New York: Harcourt Brace Jovanovich, 1979).

3. James A. Banks, "Ethnicity: Implications for Curriculum Development and Teaching," in *Cultural Issues in Education: A Book of Readings* (Los Angeles: National Multilingual Multicultural Materials Development Center, 1978).

4. Tomás A. Arciniega, "The Challenge of Multicultural Education for Teacher Educators," *Journal of Research and Development in Education* 11, no. 1 (Fall 1977).

5. Ibid.

6. Henry Trueba and Carol Barnett-Mizrahi, eds. *Bilingual Multicultural Education and the Professional: From Theory to Practice* (Rowley, Mass.: Newbury House, 1979).

7. Wallace E. Lambert, "The Effects of Bilingualism on the Individual: Cognitive and Sociocultural Consequences," in *Bilingualism: Social and Psychological Implications,* ed. Peter A. Hornby (New York: Academic Press, 1977).

8. Alberto Ochoa and Ana Maria Rodriguez, "Socio-Cultural Forces Which Affect the Self-Direction and Self-Responsibility of Students," in *Moving Toward Self-Directed Learning,* ed. Delmo Della-Dora (Washington, D.C.: Association for Supervision and Curriculum Development, April 1979), chap. 4.

CHAPTER 6

Cognitive Styles: Implications for Multiethnic Education

Barbara G. Cox and Manuel Ramírez III

Do minority students have a "style of learning" that is different from mainstream students? Are minority students really any different from other students in the way they learn? If such differences do exist, how have they developed? What can or should educators do to be responsive to these differences?

The concept of cognitive or learning styles of minority and other students is one easily oversimplified and misunderstood or misinterpreted. Unfortunately, it has been used to stereotype minority students or to further label them rather than to identify individual differences that are educationally meaningful. One of the purposes of this chapter is to examine some of the assumptions concerning cognitive styles and minority students, and to point toward some useful ways of applying the construct in multiethnic education.

Research reported by Ramírez and Castañeda,[1] Kagan and Buriel,[2] Keogh, Welles, and Weiss,[3] and others indicates that *on the average* young Mexican-American, Black, and some other minority students are more group-oriented, more sensitive to (and distracted by) the social environment, and more positively responsive to adult modeling than are non-minority students. Some research has shown that these behaviors, elsewhere grouped and labeled "field-sensitive," often appear together and describe a general approach to learning. Furthermore, research data describes minority students as, on the average, less competitive; less sensitive to spatial incursions by others; less comfortable in trial-and-error situations; and less interested in fine details of concepts, materials, or tasks that are nonsocial. These behaviors also often appear together and describe a "field-independent" approach to learning. In other words, minority students frequently show a less field-independent orientation to learning than do mainstream students.

Recognition and identification of these average differences have had both positive and negative effects in education. The positive effect has been the development of an awareness of the types of learning that our public schools tend to foster—more often field-independent and discovery-oriented than field-sensitive and demonstration-oriented or even mixed in approaches. This awareness may be one of the first steps toward improving instruction for individual students. In addition, the fact that minority students may more often display preferences for field-sensitive learning approaches has underscored one of the ways in which public education has not been responsive to minority students and has documented an important need in our attempts to provide culturally appropriate and multicultural education.

The dissemination of research information on cognitive styles has also had a negative effect in some cases, arising primarily from common problems associated with looking at mean differences; that is, by using averages to describe differences between groups, the dangers of stereotyping are more likely. The great diversity within any culture is ignored, and a construct which should be used as a *tool* for individualization becomes yet another label for categorizing and evaluating. Furthermore, the theoretical construct seems to have been applied in some cases without regard for the contribution of subject matter and situation to the student's learning behaviors. In other words, the situational aspects that may contribute significantly to the variance have not always been examined sufficiently when applying the construct in educational practice.

Not the least of the potential contributions of cognitive styles research to multiethnic education is a framework for viewing and responding to the diversity within as well as between cultures. Such a framework will assist in implementing a program that respects individual differences and learning preferences in interactions with subject matter, situation, and educational staffing.

Ramírez and Castañeda discussed this framework as an important means of validating and respecting cultural as well as individual differences in their model of cultural effects on socialization and consequently on learning style preferences.[4] Clearly, the development of a set of learning preferences is a complicated matter. However, it is not unreasonable to expect child socialization to contribute to this development. The Ramírez and Castañeda model focuses on child socialization variables and the effects of culture on socialization practices or styles. Take, for example, the types of concept development that families may encourage in their children. One family may emphasize the importance of people—how people relate to each other, who does what in the family. Children in this family may learn a lot about motivation—why people do certain things. When they learn about such things as cooking, cars, vacuum cleaners, or sewing machines, they may learn their functions in relation to how people use them. These children may learn many things by modeling what they see older people doing.

Another family may encourage their children to find out things for themselves at an early age. Children from such families learn to work out things for themselves by trial and error and will enjoy "experiments" with materials—but they may not enjoy learning concepts which require careful and exact observation and imitation. They may not learn to feel themselves a part of a group as early as will the children from the family that encourages more field-sensitive learning.

Clearly, the task, the situation, and the materials influence the ways that children are encouraged to learn or behave, and few families encourage only field-independent or field-sensitive learning, even though on the average they may use one type of strategy more than the other. The predominant or general teaching style of a family may thus be of basic importance in deciding the direction a child's learning preferences may take. Insofar as these teaching styles reflect a certain set of values held by parents and family, values that in many cases are clearly culturally determined, one may posit that cultural differences in learning style preferences develop through children's early experiences.

| CULTURAL VALUES | influence | SOCIALIZATION PRACTICES | which influence | WAYS CHILDREN PREFER TO LEARN |

IMPLICATIONS FOR TEACHING

What goals can a cognitive styles framework help multiethnic education achieve? What are some ways to accomplish these goals? Two major goals form the core of such a framework in multiethnic education: (1) to utilize and extend the strengths and learning characteristics that each student has developed through previous experience by providing learning situations that reinforce the individual's preferred or familiar ways of learning; (2) to help the student become more comfortable and successful functioning in situations and ways that he or she has not previously experienced. The former may be called "providing for students' preferred learning styles"; the latter may be called "encouraging learning-style flexibility," or "developing bicognitive functioning."

FIGURE 1
PLANNED PROVISION OF DIVERSE LEARNING EXPERIENCES

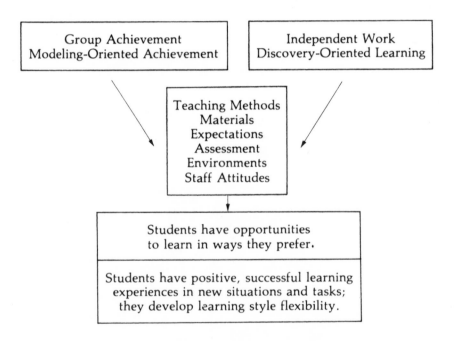

This framework has been used at several preschool and elementary school sites to implement a learning-style aspect of multiethnic education. The following is a summary of the process that has been field tested.

1. Assess students' preferred ways of learning and the way(s) in which student behaviors change from situation to situation.

2. Plan learning experiences that address conceptual goals or skills or other objectives that incorporate the student's preferred ways of

learning, using teaching methods, incentives, materials, and situations that are planned according to student preferences.

3. Implement the learning experiences that were planned.

4. Evaluate the learning experiences in terms of attainment of conceptual or other goals as well as in terms of observed student behaviors and involvement.

5. As the year progresses, plan and implement student participation in learning experiences that require behaviors the student has previously avoided. Incorporate only one aspect at a time of the total experience from the less familiar behaviors—focusing on only the reward, the materials, the situation, or the task requirements— so that the student utilizes what is familiar and comfortable or motivating as support for the newer learning experience aspects.

6. Continue to provide familiar, comfortable, successful experiences as well as to gradually introduce the children to learning in new ways.

Student behaviors, teaching behaviors, and curriculum characteristics that can be assessed and used for planning this program appear in Figures 2, 3, and 4.

We would like to comment here that this process represents a distinct departure from earlier assessment methods in work dealing with cognitive styles. Earlier methods relied heavily on research tools such as the embedded figures tests and portable rod and frame test. Such measures do not meet predictive requirements that would make them useful in educational settings; also, they assume that there exists a valid unidimensional construct that has explanatory value, an assumption which is questionable. However, the developers of these programs recommend the use of direct observation and classroom experience for assessment and planning for addressing goals in learning styles.

The process described here has been included as an important aspect of a bilingual, multicultural program in preschool through third grade classes. In this program, the cognitive styles framework has been used to develop self-awareness for administrators, teachers, and staff, as well as to work toward the goals specified for children. The cultural backgrounds of the children were respected and used through other strategies as well, including multiethnic social studies curricula and use of Spanish and English for instruction. At the preschool level, the model is in its second year of implementation in south Texas and southern California and is being evaluated.[5] At the elementary level, the program has been implemented for several years in a southern California community. Data from evaluations of this program show that by the end of third grade, math scores of children who participated were six months ahead of those of children of comparable backgrounds in a school without the program. Furthermore, on standardized tests of academic achievement, the participating children performed as well as, and in some cases better than, children in nonparticipating classes who were from homes of higher SES and more fluent English-speaking backgrounds. Children participating in the program have shown annual improvement in self-esteem and respect for cultural diversity, while teachers and staff implementing the program have shown increasing sensitivity to and awareness of individual differences among children.[6,7]

CONCLUSION

While the application of the field-independence, field-sensitivity cognitive styles construct in multiethnic education has potential for important contributions and systematic change, the greatest care must be taken to use the concepts as tools for growth and individualization and to avoid their use as labels or stereotypes. Field-independence and field-sensitivity are not undimensional, although they were so treated in the early work on the subject. Furthermore, direct evaluation of student preferences, motivating influences, and study or learning approaches by observation and classroom experience is the preferred mode of assessment, rather than the use of research tools and tests that typified most of the early work. Various ways of applying the concepts in multiethnic situations need to be developed, described, and documented in order to provide evidence of applicability in differing multiethnic situations and communities, with different teachers and staffing patterns, and differing task or curricular requirements. Finally, in order to ensure the success and advantages of multiethnic education, its goals must be approached from many perspectives and approaches.

FIGURE 2
OBSERVABLE STUDENT BEHAVIORS

Date of Observation_____

FIELD-SENSITIVE	FIELD-INDEPENDENT

RELATIONSHIP TO PEERS

1. Likes to work with others to achieve a common goal. ☐	1. Prefers to work independently. ☐
2. Likes to assist others. ☐	2. Likes to compete and gain individual recognition. ☐
3. Is sensitive to feelings and opinions of others. ☐	3. Task-oriented; is inattentive to social environment when working. ☐

PERSONAL RELATIONSHIP TO TEACHER

1. Openly expresses positive feelings for teacher. ☐	1. Avoids physical contact with teacher. ☐
2. Asks questions about teacher's tastes and personal experiences; seeks to become like teacher. ☐	2. Formal: interactions with teacher are restricted to tasks at hand. ☐

INSTRUCTIONAL RELATIONSHIP TO TEACHER

1. Seeks guidance and demonstration from teacher. ☐	1. Likes to try new tasks without teacher's help. ☐
2. Seeks rewards which strengthen relationship with teacher. ☐	2. Impatient to begin tasks; likes to finish first. ☐
3. Is highly motivated when working individually with teacher. ☐	3. Seeks nonsocial rewards. ☐

THINKING STYLE

1. Functions well when objectives are carefully explained or modeled prior to activity or lesson. ☐	1. Focuses on details and parts of things. ☐
2. Deals well with concepts in humanized or story format. ☐	2. Deals well with math and science concepts. ☐
3. Functions well when curriculum content is made relevant to personal interests and experiences. ☐	3. Likes discovery or trial-and-error learning. ☐

CODE: NEVER☐   SELDOM◪   SOMETIMES◣   USUALLY◼

FIGURE 3
CURRICULUM CHARACTERISTICS

FIELD-SENSITIVE	*FIELD-INDEPENDENT*
1. Materials readily lend themselves to fantasy, humor, and humanization.	1. Materials draw attention to factual details.
2. Relevant—teacher and students can easily relate personal experiences to curriculum.	2. Materials have high intrinsic appeal; although irrelevant to personal experiences, concepts are sufficiently interesting in and of themselves to sustain student interest.
3. Materials "invite" expressions of feelings from both teacher and students.	3. Materials require a high degree of concentration and methodical attention to subtle detail.
4. Design or format of materials is suitable for cooperative efforts and group projects.	4. Materials are more suitable for individual effort and competition than for cooperative group work.
5. Main principles and solutions are easy for teacher to demonstrate and model; materials given to students call for application of principles.	5. Materials stimulate students to search on their own for generalizations and unique solutions.
6. Lessons prefaced with supportive assurances from teacher and detailed overview of objectives.	6. Lessons prefaced with factual information and reminders of individual effort.
7. Students' attention is drawn to generalizations and global characteristics ("the big picture").	7. Students' attention directed to individual elements and ways of combining these to reach conclusions and generalizations.
8. Curriculum is humanized and adapted to students' personal experiences.	8. Curriculum focuses on factual details.

FIGURE 4
Teaching Behaviors

FIELD-SENSITIVE   *FIELD-INDEPENDENT*

CATEGORY: Instructional Behaviors

1. Express confidence in student's ability to succeed.

1. Encourage independent student achievement; emphasize importance of individual effort.

2. Give guidance to students; make purpose of activities obvious.

2. Encourage competition.

3. Encourage learning through modeling; ask students to imitate what you say or do.

3. Adopt a consultant role; encourage students to seek help only when they experience difficulty.

4. Encourage cooperation and development of group feeling; encourage students to think and work as a group.

4. Encourage learning through exploration and discovery.

5. Provide opportunities for students to see how the activities are related to their personal experiences.

5. Encourage task orientation; focus student attention on assigned tasks.

CATEGORY: Thinking Style

1. Before beginning an activity, ensure that students understand the "performance objectives," that is, give an overview or show a sample of what they will be doing.

1. Focus on details of curriculum materials.

2. Personalize curriculum; relate curriculum materials to your own interests and personal life as well as to those of the children.

2. Focus on facts and concepts.

3. Humanize curriculum; teach concepts through stories and anecdotes involving human (or humanized) characters in recognizable or familiar social settings.

CATEGORY: *Personal Behaviors*

1. Display physical and verbal expressions of approval and warmth.

2. Use personal rewards which strengthen relationship with students.

1. Somewhat formal in relationship with students, center attention on tasks and activities.

REFERENCES

1. M. Ramírez and A. Castañeda, *Cultural Democracy, Bicognitive Development, and Education,* (New York: Academic Press, 1974).

2. S. Kagan and R. Buriel, "Field Dependence-Independence and Mexican-American Culture and Education," in *Chicano Psychology,* ed. Joe L. Martinez, Jr. (New York: Academic Press, 1977), pp. 279–328.

3. B. K. Keogh, M. F. Welles, and A. Weiss, *Field Dependence-Independence and Problem-Solving Styles of Preschool Children,* Technical Report (Los Angeles: University of California, 1972).

4. Ramírez and Castañeda, *Cultural Democracy.*

5. M. Ramirez, B. Cox, J. Macaulay, and M. Macias, "Nuevas Fronteras de Aprendizaje: A Bilingual, Bicultural Preschool Program," Teachers' Manual and Curriculum Guide for Bicultural/Bilingual Preschool Programs, Follow Through Project, 1977–79.

6. Arce and Associates, "Follow Through Program Evaluation/Audit, 1977–78" (Santa Anna, Calif.: Arce and Associates, 1979).

7. M. Ramírez and Associates, Annual Report Series, 1971–1978. Culturally Democratic Learning Environments, Follow Through Project, University of California, Riverside and Santa Cruz.

CHAPTER 7

Language Diversity in Multiethnic Education

Muriel Saville-Troike

If multiethnic education is to succeed either in cultivating understanding and respect for social and cultural diversity, or in providing
truly equal learning opportunities for students from diverse sociocultural backgrounds, it must be essentially concerned with diversity in
language form and use. This is true because language includes among
its functions those of serving as a symbol and identifier of group membership and as the principal medium for mediating and manipulating
social relationships. Language is unique in its dual role as an intrinsic
component of culture and as a medium through which other aspects of
culture—including the content of formal education—are expressed and
transmitted.

In the identification function, speaking different languages is an
obvious marker of differential group membership. By switching languages, bilinguals often have the option of choosing which group to
identify with in a particular situation, and thus convey the metaphorical
meaning which goes along with such choice as well as whatever denota-
tive meaning is conveyed by the code itself. An example of such metaphorical switching was reported by a college student from Nepal who
used three different languages when being questioned by a border customs official: first Hindi as a "neutral" code for providing information,
then English to convey an educated and elite social status when excess

tea in her baggage was questioned by the guard and black-marketing motives implied, and finally her native language for "solidarity" with the guard when he was recognized (because of his accent in Hindi and English) as belonging to the same ethnic group. Bilinguals in the United States frequently use English (even with other speakers of their native language) in formal situations and to convey distance or status, but switch to the other language to express "solidarity" or ethnic identity.

Diversity of language within a single speech community, such as English, also provides a great deal of information about speakers' social identities, and even monolingual speakers of English (consciously or unconsciously) employ metaphorical switching between regional or social varieties or stylistic registers of the language to signal their role in a particular situation, their relationship to those they are speaking with, and the group identity they wish to convey.

On the receiving end, hearers of English (and other languages) regularly use language variables as a basis for judging others' social background, prestige, and even personality characteristics, as well as their ethnicity. Such concepts as status and role are not permanent qualities of language itself, but abstract communication symbols which are always perceived in relation to a particular social context. Children may be characterized as "good" or "bad" at least partly in terms of their language use, including not only the employment of politeness rules and "proper" vocabulary, but even features of pronunciation; for example, children who pronounce *coming* as "comin__" may be judged less well behaved or intelligent than those who say "*coming.*" Perceptions of individuals as "voluble" or "taciturn" are always in terms of cultural norms, and even expressions of pain and stress are culturally patterned —children in English speech communities learn withdrawal or anger, in Japanese nervous laughter or giggling, and in Navajo silence.

Conflicting attitudes toward language diversity create one of the greatest problems in cross-cultural communication between teachers and students (or their parents), and misunderstandings often occur for this reason. When the differences are understood, they may be used as an educational base; when they are not, they create a formidable barrier to learning. Contributing to an understanding of language diversity (not only in form, but in patterns of use) would clearly be one of the most important possible contributions of multiethnic education.

No complete inventory exists of different social rules for language usage or of different attitudes toward language even within the United States, but we can think of many examples. One is the difference in voice volume or level normally used by some Native American groups, with Indian students interpreting the non-Indian teachers' louder level as anger and hostility and the teachers interpreting the students' softer level as shyness or unfriendliness. A student who looks directly at the teacher when talking or listening is considered "honest," "direct," "straightforward" by most Anglos and "disrespectful" by many Mexican-Americans, Blacks, and Indians. The student who averts her/his eyes would be considered "respectful" by the latter and "shifty" or "dishonest" by many Anglos.

The standard middle-class English speech patterns presented as a model in school are likely to be considered effeminate and thus rejected by lower SES boys approaching adolescence, especially since these patterns are used by female teachers. The English of male teachers or of older boys is much more likely to be adopted by boys wanting to establish a male identity. Studies of the acquisition of English by Puerto Rican adolescents in New York and Mexican-Americans in Chicago document that the variety being learned and used is not the language taught in English classes, but the language of the dominant peer group in the communities—which in these cases is Black English.[1] Even very young children are aware of the function of language in establishing group identity, and use the appropriate variety to identify with friends. One of my former kindergarten students developed a lisp when a best friend lost his front teeth, and many middle-class Anglo parents found during the early years of integration in Southern states that their children were adding the nonstandard forms of some Black and Spanish-speaking classmates. (Middle-class Black parents were often distressed that their Standard-English-speaking children were being influenced by the nonstandard speech of lower SES White students.)

Classroom interaction is also affected by language diversity, including sociolinguistic rules regarding who should talk and when. The school supports the convention of talking one at a time (after raising a hand and being called on) and not interrupting; other cultures would consider that rude, a sure sign that no one was interested in what the primary speaker was saying. Some cultures feel it is inappropriate for children to talk at all in the presence of adults, and others that it is inappropriate for women to talk in the presence of men.

Mitigation techniques also differ, and students encounter many problems in our schools when they come from cultures that do not use the same ones that are accepted there. A middle-class student from the dominant culture has learned to avoid unpleasant assignments with such indirect excuses as *I'm tired. Can't I do that later?* or by nonverbal dawdling or daydreaming until the time is up. While often unsuccessful, the attempt brings no serious reproof. If a student has not learned these cultural strategies and says, *No, I won't,* or just *No*—which have essentially the same meaning—he/she may be considered belligerent or rude, and threatened with the principal's office.

Language learning for children is an integral part of their socialization; learning language is also part of learning to be a boy, or a girl, or rich, or poor, or Black, or White, or Chinese, or Basque, or Chicano, or dozens of other social roles into which the children are being enculturated. Children learn the social structure of their culture as they learn language, and learning to use appropriate linguistic forms when there is a choice is part of learning one's place in society. The set of sociolinguistic rules learned first through family interaction, then peer group and wider community, involves age, sex, and social class, as well as ethnic group and larger societal memberships.

Understanding the roles and identities which others have in the larger society thus minimally involves understanding how language diversity functions in manipulating and maintaining role-relationships, as a boundary marker between social groups, and as an instrument of social change. Ideally, such understanding in the context of multiethnic education will also involve the following:

1. *Making use of students' native languages as a medium of instruction and assessment.* When the educational context is one in which students understand little or no English, this is considered essential by proponents of bilingual education; students who cannot understand the language of instruction clearly cannot learn effectively, and instruction or support in their native language is widely accepted as necessary if they are to have equal opportunity for education.

2. *Accepting and accommodating the students' language and cultural patterns of language use.* The teacher, indeed the whole educational system, should seek to expand and enrich the existing repertoire of teaching styles and instructional activities to provide for the linguistic diversity of students. This is important not only when students speak languages other than English; the essence of the 1979 court decision against the Ann Arbor schools was that although students speaking Black English and their teachers could understand each other, lack of acceptance of and accommodation to the language differences resulted in unequal educational opportunity, in violation of the students' constitutional rights.

3. *Teaching about important and useful components of English as it is used in school and in other interactional contexts within American society.* Students should learn to expand and enrich their repertoire of language-related knowledge, skills, and behaviors, and extend their linguistic

and cultural competence. A traditionally recognized function of the school is to "prepare youth for life." However, schools have always taken a very narrow view of language as its relates to this function. Only a single "brand" of English—middle-class formal—has been recognized as legitimate, and the focus of textbooks and teaching has been on language form rather than use. Drilling on "correct" choice of verb form in fill-in-the-blank exercises contributes little to fluency in the use of sociolinguistically appropriate styles in various contexts.

The need to take language differences into account is quite obvious when teaching students with limited English proficiency, but accommodation must also be made to social and cultural differences among English speakers. Students may differ in their willingness to ask questions or volunteer information because of cultural differences in the appropriateness of these language behaviors. Teachers should both use and allow a variety of procedures, and be sensitive to which procedures are appropriate for which students, and to which differences in behaviors are due to cultural differences between groups and which to individual personality factors. Many students have been incorrectly stereotyped as "shy" because the teacher was requiring inappropriate behavior (from the perspective of the students' native language and culture). At the same time, students should be taught, at least by the secondary level, that asking questions and volunteering information is not considered inappropriate or overly aggressive in school, but rather is valued, and often rewarded with a higher grade. Teaching this, and guiding students to behave accordingly, is part of developing the language competence required in school.

Other language-related classroom procedures and behaviors may need to be explained or taught, including some which generally operate below the level of consciousness. We already recognize such behaviors as walking in line, or raising a hand to talk or ask permission to go to the bathroom, as unique to the subculture of the school, and therefore we formally teach them. But many students will also not know the more subtle sociolinguistic rules which are appropriate for school, and these, too, should be made the subject of explicit instruction. These include recognition of indirect instructions and commands (e.g., "I like the way Mary is sitting" meaning "Billy, get off the table!" or "Would you like to do your arithmetic now?" meaning "Do it!"), means of verbal mitigation ("Couldn't I do something else?" vs. "I won't do it"), and even how to prevaricate acceptably (e.g., how to make excuses) or to respond to recognized prevarication ("Couldn't there be another explanation?" instead of "That's a lie"). These patterns can be and should be taught as part of teaching school English. The teachers might designate the meaning to be conveyed (explained in the native language to bilingual students, if possible) and then teach various English forms which would express this, having students practice in role-playing activities; or the teacher might give a single English form and then interpret its possible meanings.

For older students, instruction in the use of appropriate language styles and routines in various practical settings (job interviews, telephone communication, information-seeking procedures) can be an important part of their "preparation for life." In the adult world, judgments are continually being passed on people on the basis of their use of language. The ability to style-switch appropriately in different situations, and with different audiences, is a skill which should be recognized and consciously taught. Students from different cultural and linguistic backgrounds, including nonmainstream English backgrounds, need at a minimum to know how various linguistic behaviors are perceived and interpreted in the mainsteam English-speaking community.

This knowledge needs to be imparted in as objective and sensitive a manner as possible. All instruction should begin with the premise that the native language or language variety spoken by the student is intrinsically as good and valid as the type of English which is being taught. Because the latter is the medium of the communication in the larger society, as well as the language of social control, of art, of philosophy, of human services, and of technological development, competence in its use is of great potential instrumental as well as humanistic significance, but it is no automatic panacea, and false promises or implications should be avoided. Lack of control of Standard English may leave one vulnerable to social and economic exploitation, but American history is replete with counterexamples of nonstandard-speaking leaders of industry and labor, and Ph.D.'s working as waiters and clerks. Whitney Young summed up the issue perhaps most succinctly when he once said, "I would rather say 'I is rich' than 'I am poor'."

Effective classroom management and discipline require a mutual sociolinguistic adaptation, first on the part of teachers to cultural differences among students, and then on the part of students to what behavior is considered appropriate in the subculture of the school. Teachers must recognize that even unconscious signals used in communicating classroom management expectations may not be read in the same way by students from different cultural backgrounds. "Accepting the language of the home" does not necessarily entail that everything said there should be allowed in school. Students of one ethnic group may hear cultural epithets regularly used about another group by their family or community, for instance, but these cannot be allowed at school. Part of socialization to the subculture of the school is learning what is appropriate or inappropriate verbal behavior for that context.

The social nature of language must also be taken into account in that all-important dimension—motivation for learning.

Every child learns a great deal of his or her language from the peer group. A child learns the subtle nuances of meanings of words by trial-and-error testing against other members of his or her group in actual communication. By school entry, children know most of the language they feel a need for in order to communicate with other members of their own group about everything in their culture which is important to them. The educational program must give them reasons to know more language if it is to teach them more successfully.

We should therefore provide as much opportunity for interstudent communication as possible. Programs which assign English-speaking students to one classroom and non-English speaking students to another are failing to utilize one of the most powerful psychological factors in language learning. Motivation for learning English can be fostered by the heterogeneous assignment of students to classes whenever possible, and by grouping procedures within the classrooms which will create both need and opportunity for students of different language backgrounds to talk to each other.

Placing students with varied backgrounds and needs in the same class by no means implies that they should have exactly the same classroom experiences. All teachers should strive toward meeting the individual needs of students and should adjust to varied rates of learning and levels of interest. If, for example, a class contains some students who speak Spanish but little or no English, brief periods each day should be devoted to teaching basic English sentence patterns and vocabulary to just the Spanish-speaking students. These students will learn English far more efficiently if there is opportunity throughout the rest of the school day for them to participate in varied activities in the room and on the playground with English-speaking classmates.

Language factors are critically relevant to assessment of student achievement, teacher performance, and program effectiveness. Testing is itself a communicative event, and students may perform differentially in differing testing conditions because of their language background. Evaluation instruments can seldom be considered linguistically neutral, no matter how "objective" their format.

Validity and reliability of tests should be considered language-specific. While a test may be valid for members of one language group, it may not measure what it purports to measure in another. For example, a test that has been used to "prove" that Mexican-American children have poorer auditory discrimination than Anglo children was based on the discriminations made in the sounds of the *English* phonological system. If the test had included the task of distinguishing between the sounds [r] and [r̃] (as in *pero* 'but' and *perro* 'dog') or the identity of vowels in unstressed positions, Spanish-speaking students would probably have scored higher than native English speakers; if tone, speakers of Chinese and Vietnamese; and if nasal vs. oral vowels, speakers of French.

The reliability of tests is affected not only by the ethnicity of the tester and the experience which students have had taking tests, but the type of questions (e.g., true-false questions are not widely used in Latin America), the modality of the test (written vs. oral), and the language code which is used (a Spanish test developed in Puerto Rico is not valid in California or Texas, and perhaps not even in New York). The language choice is relative to the subject area (depending on the language in which a particular subject was learned), and tests in the "native language" should take cognizance of the variety of that language which the students speak, and whether they are literate in that language. Just as English has its regional, social, and contextual varieties, so do other languages, and a test (or tester) using one variety may fail to elicit a performance on the part of the student which reflects his/her true ability. The classic demonstration of this is Labov's experiment in which an intimidating White interrogator in a school setting elicited minimal verbal response from a Black child, who later responded freely when interviewed at home by a Black interviewer.[2] Recent failures to recognize language and cultural differences among Indochinese refugee students have had sometimes unfortunate results.

When language itself becomes a focus in the instructional program, as it does in bilingual programs, it may be the case that the effect of a program results more from the affective impact of using the students' language than from the purely cognitive benefits (though both are surely relevant). Research has shown that students who attend school in their native countries (e.g., Mexico) for several years before coming to the United States tend to do better in English than those who begin school here.[3] In other words, the schools here are at least partly responsible for retarding the students (the alternative explanation—that schools elsewhere are better than U.S. schools—is unlikely).

The cause of the retardation is to be found both in the school and outside. Where schools have hired members of the students' ethnic group as regular teachers and administrators, and have developed a strong academic program which respects, utilizes, and builds upon the students' native language and culture, achievement has exceeded national norms in English, reading, and mathematics. Where the school has hired staff from the minority group only in subordinate positions, or not at all, and has given only lip service to the more superficial aspects of the group's culture—food, dress, holidays—the reality of social inequities beyond the school has been telegraphed to minority students, whose achievement has been depressed accordingly.[4] In this context, even the use of the native language may have little positive effect.

Social attitudes may thus play a powerful part in determining levels of success in language learning. In Sweden, where Finns are looked down upon and disparaged, Finnish children have great trouble learning Swedish and do poorly in school.[5] In Australia, on the other hand, where Finns are admired and respected, Finnish children usually learn English and do well in school.[6] The "Pygmalion effect" often manifests itself in our own schools, where Chinese students are expected to do well, and Hispanic or Filipino students are expected to fail—and the expectation becomes a self-fulfilling prophecy.

Since language is such a powerful symbol of personal and group identity, direct and indirect attacks on it in the classroom and outside are attacks on the students' own identities and on their perception of self-worth and the worth of family, friends, and others they admire. Direct attacks may take the form of prohibition on the use of another language, or public corrections of the form of a student's speech. Indirect attacks are often subtle, and may range from omissions of the students' language from public use (on signs, in announcements, etc.), to disparagements of its expressive power, negative evaluations of the intelligence of its users, failure to utilize it in testing or making home contacts, or restrictive pressures on its use by staff. Even where the students' language is incorporated into the curriculum, books and materials used may have an inferior appearance to the English materials, again betraying a second-class status for the other language, and by extension, for its speakers.

Education of one kind or another is always going on in the classroom—students are always learning something, whether it is what the teacher intended or not. It follows that education may be either positive or negative, and that what students learn from school may be beneficial or detrimental. Although prejudice and ethnocentrism may not be explicitly listed as objectives of the curriculum, they may be unconsciously transmitted just as surely as if they were. While minority students are learning to disvalue their language, their culture, and their social group, the majority students are likewise learning to disparage their peers and to believe in the inferiority of the minority language and culture, and the inherent superiority of the majority culture and its linguistic medium, Standard English. Such beliefs, though founded in ignorance, become deeply engrained to the point that they acquire an almost religious tenacity, and become the basis for perpetuating inequities and inequality of educational opportunity.

While schools and teachers have understandably focused much of their attention on raising the achievement level of minority students (sometimes at the expense of the students' language or culture), helping nonminority Standard-English-speaking students develop an understanding of the nature of language and linguistic diversity should also form an important part of the educational program. While the school must prepare students for coping with the society into which it is graduating them, it can and should contribute to improving the society of the future as it prepares today's students to become tomorrow's adults. Mirabeau B. Lamar, president of the Republic of Texas, said that "An educated mind is the guiding genius of democracy"; teaching respect for linguistic diversity so that it comes to be considered a characteristic of the educated mind can thus form a major contribution of multiethnic education to preserving the future of American democracy.

REFERENCES

1. Walt Wolfram, *Sociolinguistic Aspects of Assimilation: Puerto Rican English in New York City* (Arlington, Va.: Center for Applied Linguistics, 1974).

2. William Labov, "The Logic of Non-Standard English," in *Linguistics and the Teaching of Standard English to Speakers of Other Languages or Dialects,* GURT 22, ed. James E. Alatis (Washington, D.C.: Georgetown University Press, 1970), pp. 1–44.

3. Rudolph C. Troike, "Research Evidence for the Effectiveness of Bilingual Education," *NABE Journal* 3, no. 1 (1978): 13–24.

4. Elizabeth Cohen, unpublished research cited by Courtney Cazden at the National Association of Bilingual Education Conference, Seattle, 1979.

5. Tove Skutnabb-Kangas and Pertti Toukamaa, *Teaching Migrant Children's Mother Tongue and Learning the Language of the Host Country in the Context of the Socio-Cultural Situation of the Migrant Family* (Helsinki: Finnish National Commission for UNESCO, 1976).

6. Teija Ilpola, "Australian Suomalainen Arvostettu: Kieliolotkin Kohentumassa" (The Finns in Australia Rated Highly), *Suomi Silta* 2 (1979): 8, 9.

CHAPTER 8

Becoming an Effective Cross-Cultural Counselor
Cherry A. Banks

Counseling touches all of our lives. We counsel and are counseled by friends, relatives, and even strangers. Our philosophies and styles may differ, but we are all involved in interpersonal communication. We share with the professional counselor the desire to extend ourselves and to help. This chapter discusses the qualities and skills necessary to become an effective professional counselor in today's multiethnic society. It has important implications, however, for all professional educators and lay counselors.

THE COUNSELING RELATIONSHIP

The relationship between counselor and client is of utmost importance in interpersonal helping. By building a rapport, these two individuals begin to know and relate to each other as unique persons. Their relationship serves as a vehicle for a better understanding so that when the real problems facing the client are identified, they begin to work on them. The quality of the relationship is very important in cross-cultural counseling. However, in order to establish better relationships with individuals from diverse ethnic and racial groups, cross-cultural counselors also require a sophisticated understanding of ethnic cultures, effective cross-cultural communication skills, and an ability to communicate caring and positive attitudes to their clients.

Basic Attitudinal Ingredients in Effective Counseling

Carl Rogers has identified three basic attitudinal ingredients that are essential for effective counseling: empathy, genuineness, and (unconditional) positive regard.[1] Ethnic isolation and cultural conditioning, however, can make it difficult for counselors to communicate these attitudes to people who are culturally and racially different from themselves. Because many Americans are socialized within isolated ethnic communities lacking opportunities to know and relate to people from diverse ethnic and cultural groups, such isolated experiences frequently result in misconceptions and stereotypes about ethnic and racial groups.

In many ways we are a nation of strangers. Although we live in the same time and space, often we do not have an appreciation or understanding of our common humanity and destiny. Too frequently, our mental, spiritual, and social isolation results in distrust, misunderstanding, and rivalry. Without special cross-cultural counseling skills, therefore, most counselors may find that their ethnic isolation and cultural conditioning will make it very difficult for them to experience empathy, genuineness, and (unconditional) positive regard for their ethnic clients.[2]

Empathy. Empathic understanding requires counselors to put themselves in their clients' place and see their clients' problems as their own. Counselors who lack a diversified cultural background often can examine and understand problems only from their own limited frames of reference. They may be unable to see problems from their clients' perspectives. Moreover, they may be unable to gain a clear understanding and appreciation of their clients' feelings or the complexity of the situations they face. Such counselors will most likely be seen by clients as uncaring or lacking the ability to understand their problems.

Genuineness. This quality is an important ingredient in the counseling relationship. To be genuine counselors must present themselves as they really are. They must be sincere. Those who have not examined their own psychodynamic and cultural conditioning may feign interest and concern for their clients, but such counselors present a false image and will usually be perceived by the client as insincere. On the other hand, genuineness does not always have a positive effect on the counseling relationship. It is possible for a counselor to communicate genuine feelings that are perceived negatively by the client. Counselors who are genuine but who have negative feelings about their clients or their

172393

clients' ethnic group will find it difficult to establish a positive relationship with them. Such counselors need to clarify their feelings about race and ethnicity, and try to gain an understanding of their real meanings. *Unconditional Positive Regard.* This attitude requires counselors to prize their clients for what they are without judging them. They must accept their clients as they are at the moment, not as they were yesterday or as they may be tomorrow. Counselors must be prepared to accept both the angry and the positive feelings of their clients. When they relate to clients in such an unconditionally caring fashion, they can help them begin to see themselves in a more positive way. Unconditional positive regard can help awaken untold potentialities in clients. This attitude, however, can be especially difficult to establish in cross-cultural counseling relationships. Widespread misconceptions based on negative attitudes and beliefs about the nature of race and ethnicity in our society often cause counselors to make inaccurate judgments about individuals based on ethnic or racial group membership.

The cross-cultural counselor must be willing and able to explore and question negative attitudes and beliefs about ethnic groups and ethnic clients. Without a sophisticated understanding of race and ethnicity in American society, the counselor may confuse societal problems with the client's problems and believe that the client must experience total assimilation before she or he will be acceptable.

Transference and Countertransference

Counseling does not occur in a vacuum; it occurs within a societal context. Both counselor and client are affected by many variables within society. While these variables occur outside the counseling relationship, they can profoundly affect it. The process and influence of these societal variables on the counseling relationship are best described by the concepts of transference and countertransference.

Transference involves the development of a positive or negative emotion by the client toward the counselor based on past experiences. Ethnicity and race can play a role in the kinds of experiences the client has had and his/her response to the race and ethnicity of the counselor. Some ethnic minority clients may find it difficult to trust an Anglo counselor for many reasons, including past experiences with racial discrimination and racism. Counselors may find feelings of anger and hostility directed toward them because clients perceive them as roadblocks to their success. Some Anglo clients may experience cognitive dissonance with an ethnic minority counselor. They may feel uncomfortable with such a counselor because they have internalized many of the societal myths about the behavior, values, and skills of ethnic minorities. Such clients may doubt that an ethnic minority counselor has the skills and knowledge needed to help them.

Counselors transfer their feelings from past experiences to their present relationships with clients during countertransference. Some counselors may find that through the years they have developed certain ideas about ethnic minority clients and use them when working with new clients. Such counselors may be in touch with their past experiences but out of touch with their present clients. This condition can lead to inappropriate behavior and can strain the counseling relationship.

It is reasonable to assume that transference and countertransference may occur during counseling. These processes do not necessarily prevent effective counseling between counselors and clients of different ethnic and racial groups, however. Transference and countertransference can also occur with counselors and clients who are members of the same ethnic and racial groups. Such counselors and clients frequently have different levels of ethnic identity, ethnic behavior, values, world views, and socioeconomic status. Because of the possibility of transference and countertransference in any counseling relationship, counselors must be aware of this potential, recognize these processes when they occur, and use them to move the counseling process and their own personal growth forward.

Values in Counseling

Though often unrecognized, values strongly affect the counseling relationship and are an integral part of the process. Counselors' values are reflected in their philosophies, their methods, their use of test scores, and their conceptions of what is mentally healthy. Counselors' value orientations help determine the goals and behaviors they encourage or discourage. Because a client's life goal may be limited or misdirected by the values reflected in inappropriate counseling and testing, the counseling process should directly or indirectly explore each client's values, helping each person sort out and actualize them. To help clients do this, counselors must be willing and able to explore, question, and clarify their own values. In this way, they will be better prepared to identify and work on value conflicts that may occur between them and their clients. The effective cross-cultural counselor appreciates helping the client live in ways congruent with his/her own values, realizing that the values of others cannot be forced on the client.

Communication

The responsibility for establishing meaningful communication with clients lies primarily with the counselor. Counselors cannot assume that just because they feel they are sincere, accepting, and empathetic their clients perceive such attitudes. Their attitudes, beliefs, and values should be communicated to clients in ways that can be understood within different cultural contexts. To communicate effectively, counselors must understand the dynamics of cross-cultural communication and use their knowledge to help direct their behavior.

Communication involves a process of exchanging information between individuals who interpret symbols and behavior similarly. Problems occur in communicating across cultures in the United States because although we share many similarities in patterns of behavior, we have many subtle differences in the interpretation of behavior in the various ethnic cultures. Lack of attention to certain nuances in behavior clues may lead us to believe that we are in complete communication when we are not. Communication can break down abruptly and misunderstandings can occur when an individual behaves in a way that is quite acceptable in his/her culture but not in another ethnic culture or in the mainstream American culture. Without special skills and knowledge, most counselors will be unable to effectively communicate with individuals who do not interpret symbols and behaviors as they do. Attempting to bridge the communication gap or to prove that one is culturally literate by using slang or an inaccurate form of the client's language or dialect will most likely be insulting to the client and considered patronizing.

Most personal communication is nonverbal. It is estimated that about 65 percent of all face-to-face communication does not involve speech. Touching, physical space, voice tone and volume, gestures, and use of the eyes are different ways of communicating nonverbally. Each has specific and often diverse meanings in different cultures. Counselors who are unaware of what is appropriate and normative within other ethnic cultures may unwittingly use their own cultural norms as the standard for judging behavior in cross-cultural contexts.

THE DIVERSITY WITHIN ETHNIC CULTURES

The nature of the counseling relationship requires that counselors relate to individuals, not to generalized groups. When attention is focused on group norms, there is a risk of losing sight of the *individual,* and perhaps viewing the individual as part of a monolithic group. It is unproductive and a misapplication of the concept of culture to assume that all members of an ethnic group are culturally homogeneous. Such a false assumption can cause the counselor to perceive the client as a stereotypic representation of her/his ethnic culture rather than as an individual with unique characteristics. A response to individual members of an ethnic group based on a composite and often stereotypic picture of the group can lead to misunderstandings and anger.

The misuse of the concept of culture generally results from too little rather than too much information about ethnic cultures. A sophisticated understanding of the relationship between individuals and their cultures, on the other hand, requires an in-depth study of the nature of ethnicity in American society, the concept of race, and the experiences of ethnic groups in the United States.

By using their knowledge of both culture and the individual client, cross-cultural counselors can become more effective. Their knowledge should include an awareness of the complexity of ethnic cultures and the diversity within them, and an appreciation of the limits of cultural knowledge as an explanation of individual behavior. They also need a sophisticated understanding of the tremendous cultural diversity *within* ethnic groups, recognizing the wide range of possible responses and combinations among *group* cultural components and the *personalities* of individual group members. In addition, they should take care not to overgeneralize the cultural components of an ethnic group to all of its members.

Reducing Prejudice

Cross-cultural counselors should not only be prepared to work with individuals from diverse ethnic cultures, they should also be prepared to help clients reduce their racial and ethnic prejudices. An unhealthy attitude that is widespread in our society, racial prejudice has pronounced effects on the prejudiced individual as well as on its victims. Since the 1960's our society has made some progress in reducing institutionalized discrimination and segregation. More than in the past, individuals of different ethnic groups are now likely to have direct contact. But for highly prejudiced persons, seeing successful ethnic minorities in positions of authority or in equal-status situations and interacting with them, for example, can be very difficult. Thus there is a need for the cross-cultural counselor to help individuals reduce their negative attitudes, beliefs, and behavior.

Individuals who have weak racial and ethnic biases are more likely to discard their negative beliefs and attitudes than are those who have tenacious ones. For persons with great intolerance, prejudice usually has much functional significance. Their attitudes and beliefs are often deep and highly resistant to change. People commonly use three processes to resist changing prejudiced attitudes and beliefs: *selective perception, avoidance,* and *group support.* [3]

In selective perception, individuals organize their view of the world to prevent a conflict between their attitudes and the information they acquire. When they have a new experience, their interpretation allows them to fit it into their existing cosmos. Prejudiced individuals often use selective perception to dismiss positive information that does not confirm their stereotypic beliefs about ethnic groups.

Prejudiced individuals also tend to avoid information that contradicts their beliefs. Avoidance can take many forms. A person who opposes ethnic studies programs, for example, may be required to attend a lecture on the need for such programs in the schools. He or she may refuse to accept the information presented, however, or may "hear" the speaker make controversial statements that other individuals in the audience do not hear.

By limiting most of their contacts to persons within their own ethnic and racial group, individuals are often able to avoid changing or examining their biased attitudes and beliefs. Social groups offer emotional support and a feeling of belonging. They can also reinforce beliefs and attitudes about outside ethnic and racial groups.

Once the counselor is aware of the processes a client uses to maintain prejudices, she or he can communicate that awareness. This can be the beginning of the client's understanding of personal behaviors and attitudes. The counselor can present cases involving prejudiced attitudes and behaviors to discuss and investigate for solutions. Role playing can also be an effective technique. It can help the biased client gain insight into personal behaviors and attitudes by providing an opportunity to explore the feelings and perspectives of individuals from different ethnic and racial groups.

Sensitivity training can also help clients reduce prejudice if it is directed by a well-trained and skilled leader. This technique involves small group discussions where members are encouraged to candidly express their feelings and concerns.

Under certain circumstances, direct contact between members of racial and ethnic groups can help reduce prejudice. To be effective, direct contact should involve members of ethnic or racial groups who are of equal status with the client.[4] These contact situations should also be rewarding and pleasant. The probability of reducing prejudice will increase if individuals of different racial and ethnic groups work together to achieve common goals.

HOW TO BECOME A MORE EFFECTIVE CROSS-CULTURAL COUNSELOR

Cross-cultural counseling involves a number of skills that can be learned. Counselors who are willing to devote the time and energy necessary to acquire these skills can increase their level of cross-cultural competency. Such skill improvement involves three processes: (1) self-examination, (2) gaining insight and planning for the future, and (3) taking the necessary risks to change one's behavior and putting the plan into action. The plan of action is a personal one, varying from individual to individual. It is open-ended, allowing one to start wherever one is today to increase one's skills. Moreover, it encourages personal growth, building on the skills being acquired.

Phase I. Self-Examination

Examining who you are and how you arrived at this point is a difficult task. It requires the asking of some hard questions and an honest search for answers. To begin this process, take a critical look at your ability to function as a cross-cultural counselor. Where are your informational gaps? Do you have a sophisticated understanding of ethnicity and race in the United States? What do you know about the histories and cultural experiences of ethnic groups in the United States? Review some of your recent counseling experiences. How do you feel about the level of communication, empathy, and genuineness you were able to establish with your ethnic clients? Do you feel you were able to help the clients? Next, look at your school. Do the attitudes and behaviors of parents, students, teachers, or administrators have any implications for cross-cultural counseling?

Phase II. Insight and Planning

In this phase you are beginning to acquire an understanding of the skills, attitudes, and behaviors you need to work on. Next, reach out and touch bases with some other people to expand and validate your understanding of your situation. Talk to students, parents, and colleagues at school to find out how they feel about how you are functioning and how you can help them in your role as a cross-cultural counselor. This process will give you a better idea of how you can serve your school as well as some ideas on local resources and support; it will also let the school community know that you are concerned and available for help. Then, review your information from the school community and your original ideas about your level of functioning as a cross-cultural counselor. State in your own words how you feel you should function in this role. This is your personal definition of cross-cultural counseling.

Make a list of all the things you can begin to do immediately to improve your abilities as a cross-cultural counselor. For example, you might include such items as refusing to make assumptions about a client's background or ability based on race or ethnic group. Next, list all the goals you plan to work on along with the resources you will use to attain them, such as becoming more familiar with ethnic minority cultures by taking courses or workshops on ethnic cultures at the local college or university. Rank order your goals, placing those needing the least amount of work at the top and those requiring the most work at the bottom of a list.

Phase III. Taking Risks and Acting

Changing behavior is not an easy task. People are usually rather comfortable and skilled in their old behaviors. New behaviors are risky and unknown, and it is reasonable to feel uncomfortable or afraid when learning them. In this phase you are aware of what should be done and how to go about it. Now it is time to take action. You can begin slowly and thoughtfully by organizing your goals in a *growth notebook*. On the outside of the notebook write your definition of cross-cultural counseling. On separate pages in the notebook enter each goal (starting at the top of your list) and the information on how you plan to achieve it. Start with your easiest goal on page one and work your way through the notebook. Each day do at least one thing to work toward your goal, entering it in the notebook. Also note your reflections on the way(s) your actions have affected your knowledge, attitudes, and/or effectiveness. Note changes that friends, colleagues, and students mention they see in you. After your program is underway, you may find that you need to reconceptualize, expand, or delete certain parts.

Discuss what you are doing with colleagues who are interested in cross-cultural counseling. Some colleagues might like to participate in a similar program, and you may be able to start a group that can offer important support. You can also use this program when working with clients who want to achieve specific goals.

CROSS-CULTURAL COUNSELING: A PROCESS

Cross-cultural counselors are involved in a process of self-examination, training, and practice. They are attempting to increase their knowledge, and to improve their ability to be open, trusting, spontaneous, flexible, caring, and understanding with individuals from diverse ethnic and racial groups (see Figure 1). They are aware of the impact of their behavior on their clients and of their own problems in dealing with race and ethnicity. Their attempt to solve these problems in their own lives helps them become more effective with clients.

Cross-cultural counselors recognize the vast diversity of experi-

FIGURE 1
CHARACTERISTICS OF THE EFFECTIVE CROSS-CULTURAL COUNSELOR

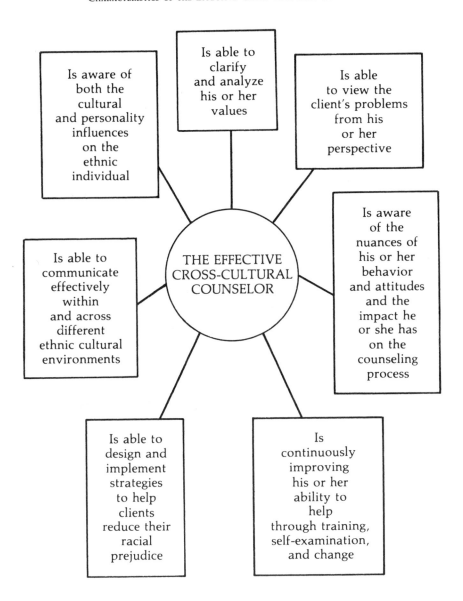

ences, cultural forms, goals, perspectives, and realities that exist *among* and *within* American ethnic groups. They feel comfortable with themselves and with individuals from diverse racial and ethnic groups. They are involved in a process that requires them to experience other cultures and to be open to those experiences. These attitudes and experiences equip them to work with and help individuals from diverse racial and ethnic groups. In moving outside their own cultures, effective cross-cultural counselors are able to view other cultures from the perspectives of outsiders and to function effectively in diverse cultural settings. Thus they are better able to understand their own culture and themselves because of their ability to function well in other cultures. Becoming an effective cross-cultural counselor does not occur overnight. It is an ongoing process, not a state of being.

REFERENCES

1. Carl R. Rogers, "The Interpersonal Relationship: The Core of Guidance," in *Guidance: An Examination,* eds. Ralph L. Mosher, Richard F. Carle, and Chris D. Kehas (New York: Harcourt, Brace and World, 1965), pp. 49–65.

2. Clemmont E. Vontress, "Counseling Blacks," *Personnel and Guidance Journal* 48, no. 9 (May 1970): 713–19.

3. Gordon W. Allport, *The Nature of Prejudice* (Reading, Mass.: Addison-Wesley, 1954).

4. Allport, *The Nature of Prejudice.*

CHAPTER 9

Testing and Assessment Practices in Multiethnic Education

Jane R. Mercer

TESTING AND SCHOOLING: A HISTORICAL OVERVIEW

Testing and schooling are so closely interwoven that it is not possible to understand standardized testing without first comprehending the nature of schooling in American society. During the colonial era, English settlers gradually achieved military and economic dominance, pushing the French into Canada, supplanting the Dutch in New York, and dispossessing the Native Americans. Then they set about establishing a society which would be a replica of England with English as the universal language and economic, religious, and family institutions patterned after those in England.

Following the war of independence, with the arrival of immigrants from other cultural backgrounds, the Anglo inhabitants faced the first challenge to their cultural dominance. At this time they insisted that non-Anglos learn the English language and become acculturated to Anglo ways. Their policy of Anglicization was based on the assumption of "the desirability of maintaining English institutions (as modified by the American Revolution), the English language, and English-oriented cultural patterns as dominant and standard in American life."[1] Called Americanization, this process was first implemented through "free schools" which were set up by private, paternalistic organizations of upper-class Anglo citizens in Boston and New York for the express purpose of teaching second-generation immigrants the English language and instilling in them loyalty to Anglo institutions and values. These schools were not designed for the children of the Anglo majority but were for the socialization and acculturation of the poor to the Anglo way of life.[2]

When tax-supported public education systems were later established, they adopted the Anglicization policies of the "free schools." All instruction was in English. The curriculum focused exclusively on Anglo-American institutions, history, literature, and values. Although the public schools have, officially, been religiously and politically neutral, they have always been the culture-bearer for only one of the many cultural streams brought by immigrants to this continent. From these beginnings, we have the public schools as they exist today: Anglo-centric, monocultural, biased toward middle- and upper-class customs and lifestyle, standardized, and centralized. They are huge bureaucracies administered by professional educators who have been trained in only the Anglo cultural tradition.

Although the early schools used tests, they consisted of teacher-designed instruments covering the spelling, arithmetic, and other curricular materials taught in the school. Standardized testing, as we know it today, first began in France around 1905, where Alfred Binet, in collaboration with Simon, was commissioned by the French government to design a method for identifying those children who would not benefit from the regular school program and who should be placed in special schools for the mentally subnormal.[3] Although some of their test items covered material which might be learned in school, most dealt with skills and information which they believed all French children would have had an opportunity to acquire from what Cortés has called the general "societal curriculum":[4] the knowledge, values, behaviors, language, and cognitive style learned from their socialization in the family and community. Items were grouped into age levels based on a tryout sample of normal children 3 through 13 years of age. The child's score on the scale, expressed as a "mental level," was the highest age level on the scale at which the child performed successfully. Binet and Simon assumed that all children were exposed to the same societal curriculum and that those who had not learned the curriculum must be intellectually subnormal.

In 1916, L. M. Terman at Stanford University developed an American revision of the Binet-Simon scale known as the Stanford-Binet. Translating Binet's test into English, he modified the question content

94

to reflect the societal curriculum of the dominant Anglo cultural group, and standardized it on White, predominantly middle-class, English-speaking children. Terman used an intelligence quotient (IQ), the ratio between mental level, or mental age, as it had come to be called, and chronological age. The intelligence quotient represented the child's performance on the test relative to the performance of other children of the same age, thus recognizing the inappropriateness of comparing the test performance of a four-year-old child with that of a nine-year-old child for purposes of inferring "intelligence." The four-year-old would have had less exposure to the societal curriculum than would the nine-year-old and such comparisons would lack normative validity.

On the 1916 version of the test girls scored higher than boys. When Terman and Merrill developed the 1937 revision of the Stanford-Binet, they assumed that girls and boys had equal "intelligence" and that the elevated scoring of girls was a deficiency in the test, a lack of normative validity. To equalize the sexes, they reduced the number of verbal tests, on which girls did better than boys, and introduced nonverbal tests, on which boys did better than girls.[5] At the same time, Terman and Merrill also discovered that rural children performed less well than urban children—with IQs of 99.2 compared to 105.7—and that there were large differences by socioeconomic status—116 for children of professional fathers compared to 98 for children of day laborers.[6] They did not engineer their test to equate rural-urban or socioeconomic differences, however, because they believed the scores reflected real differences in "intelligence." Similarly, racial differences were well known by the time of the revision but no adjustments were made for race.

Although Binet called his test a measure of "intelligence," he did not claim that his tests measured innate ability. He recognized that they measured what a child had learned, the child's achievement. John Goddard and Lewis Terman, however, the two men most responsible for bringing Binet's test to America, believed that the test measured more than learning: they believed that it measured innate ability. Furthermore, they believed that this innate ability was a highly heritable trait which would change little in the course of a lifetime.[7] Their beliefs were widely accepted.

Several decades later, test publishers began producing tests focusing more specifically on the school curriculum—on reading, math, language, and so forth—which came to be called "achievement" tests. As the use of academic achievement tests became more widespread, the belief developed that there were two kinds of tests, "intelligence tests" which measured a child's innate ability and "achievement tests" which measured what a child had learned. In fact, there is no fundamental difference between the two types of test; they draw their items from the same item pool. In one case, the same questions appear in two different tests. One is called a test of intelligence and the other a test of achievement.[8] All measure competency in the use of standard English, mathematical skills, and knowledge of the Anglo core culture. "Achievement" tests focus more specifically on the school curriculum while "intelligence" tests focus more on the societal curriculum of the Anglo-American mainstream, but both are measures of what a child has learned, and both are simply subtests of one large test that measures the child's acculturation to and familiarity with the Anglo core culture.

With this brief historical overview, let us now discuss the four purposes for which tests are used in education today.

PURPOSES OF TESTING IN TODAY'S SCHOOLS

There are four major purposes for the use of tests in American education: to guide the instructional process; to screen for possible organic problems; to evaluate a student's academic performance compared to that of other students in some normative sample; and to estimate the student's "intelligence." Each purpose requires different types of tests based on different assessment frameworks. The definition of what constitutes a "valid" test varies with the purpose for which the test is being used; so also does the determination of whether the test is racially or culturally discriminatory. A source of great confusion in educational testing is the failure to differentiate these four purposes and the attempt to use a single assessment framework, a single definition of test "validity," and a single definition of what constitutes racial and cultural discrimination for all four functions.

Testing to Guide the Instructional Process

Teacher-constructed tests designed to cover curricular materials are examples of testing used to guide the instructional process. In recent years, a large number of "criterion-referenced" tests have been developed by various organizations and publishers. They yield information on the student's current skill or knowledge in a particular graded curriculum. The teacher can use test information to determine the next stage in the instructional process for the particular student. Carver has called this the "edumetric" function of tests.[9] Typically, the teacher is interested in the raw score, the actual number of items passed. The score is compared with a series of graded criteria incorporated in the curriculum.

It is anticipated that the student's raw scores will improve with instruction. Hence edumetric tests are the appropriate type of test to use in evaluating the effectiveness of educational programs.

Because present edumetric tests are an integral part of the present school curriculum, they reflect the monocultural, monolingual, Anglocentric characteristics of that curriculum. Development of multilingual and multicultural curricula will require dramatic extensions of present testing practices to cover new academic areas. In a truly bilingual program, students would take edumetric tests in more than one language. In a truly multicultural school, students would take tests covering the language, values, institutions, and history of numerous cultural streams. The decision concerning the nature of the curriculum is, essentially, a political decision. When the goals of education are expanded, edumetric testing will become multilingual and multicultural. If the testing is culturally limited, it is because the curriculum is culturally limited.

An edumetric test has content validity to the extent that it accurately mirrors what is being taught. It has pragmatic validity to the extent that it accurately identifies those students who have or have not mastered a particular curriculum. It is racially and culturally nondiscriminatory to the extent that it is equally proficient in measuring the competencies of students from differing racial and cultural backgrounds in a particular curriculum. The fact that students from some groups may be less proficient in a particular curriculum and tests of that curriculum than students from other groups is not evidence that the tests, per se, are at fault. The source of the differences is more fundamental and rests, at least in part, with a limited curriculum that represents the cultural tradition of only one group. Students less familiar with that tradition will do less well in the curriculum and less well on criterion-referenced tests based on that curriculum. When the curriculum is changed, the tests will change. The relative proficiency of different groups may also change.

Testing to Screen for Organic Problems

For many children, difficulties with vision, hearing, motor coordination, and other biological problems are first identified in the school. Although educators usually do not include screening for organic problems as one of the purposes of testing in public education, it makes little sense to conduct elaborate educational testing on a child who is having academic difficulty without first checking to see that the child is an intact organism. If the child has organic problems, then some type of medical intervention may be required before educational progress is possible.

Tests for the presence of organic anomalies are conducted within the medical model, which has also been called the pathological model and the deficit model. They seek to identify the symptoms of a pathological condition. Unlike edumetric tests, they are not culture-bound because the human organism is similar across cultural groups. A medical model measure is valid if it accurately identifies biological problems. We do not need to be concerned with racial or cultural discrimination when screening for organic problems, if the tests actually are measuring the organism. Difficulties arise when the only observable "symptoms" are behaviors and the presence of an organic basis cannot be specifically identified. In such cases, the burden of proof rests with the evaluator to present evidence that organic inferences are justified. Interpreting scores on IQ tests as measures of innate ability is but one example of overgeneralizing behavioral signs and imputing a biological cause without any clear evidence of organic mechanisms. Similarly, many "diagnoses" of "minimal brain dysfunction" and "learning disabilities" rest on questionable biological inferences from behavioral signs. Educators need to be wary of such interpretations and to ask for evidence of their validity.

Testing to Compare Student Performance with a Set of Norms

A third purpose of testing in present educational practice is to compare student performance on the test with that of some normative population. The raw scores are standardized to show the student's position in the distribution of scores relative to that of other students of the same age. Tests which purportedly measure "intelligence" such as the Stanford-Binet, the Wechsler Intelligence Scale for Children-Revised, and the Slosson are of this type. Standardized, norm-referenced "achievement" tests also belong in this category. Carver has called such tests "psychometric" measures,[10] or tests not tied to any particular curriculum. The so-called "intelligence" tests sample skills and information believed to be generally available in the "societal curriculum" of the Anglo core-culture child. They do not sample skills and information which would be available in the "societal curriculum" of children from other backgrounds, such as Black, Mexican-American, Puerto Rican, or Native American. The standardized "achievement" tests are more closely tied to the school curriculum. Although they embody the general educational goals of American public education as perceived by the test designers, they may or may not accurately reflect the curriculum of a particular school. Since both types of tests measure knowledge of the Anglo core-culture, their scores are highly correlated,[11] and children from such backgrounds consistently score higher on both types of tests.[12]

How have scores on standardized tests been used? First, some schools have tried to use these scores to monitor the educational progress of students. However, there are serious difficulties with this use of standardized test scores. Because the tests are age-normed, the norms with which a student is compared constantly rise as the student ages. Just to remain in the same relative position, an individual's raw scores must show continuous improvement. But a student's standard scores can remain unchanged even though s/he is making academic progress. Hence, standardized tests are less useful for measuring educational progress than are scores on edumetric measures.

Second, some schools have tried to use scores on standardized tests to evaluate the effectiveness of educational programs or to rate the effectiveness of teachers. Because of the age norming, programs in which students are making "normal" progress will look as if the students are standing still because their relative position will not have changed. Similarly, teachers whose students grow sufficiently to maintain their relative position will appear to be failures because the average standard scores for their classes will remain the same. In order to increase the average standard score of a group, the students must learn at a faster rate than the norm group with which they are being compared. Unfortunately, many programs have been declared failures on the basis of inappropriate evaluations with standard tests.

Third, standard tests have been used by lawmakers to identify and categorize students for the purpose of educational funding. At first glance, such a procedure seems quite reasonable. Students who score low compared to other students on skills required to succeed in school could possibly benefit from supplementary help and resources. The law has gone beyond simply using tests to identify educational needs, however. For example, Public Law 94-142, a recent federal statute, requires that a child not only be in need of special services but be certified as defective before funds are made available. Under current statutes, "the term 'handicapped children' means those children evaluated . . . as being mentally retarded, hard of hearing, deaf, speech impaired, visually handicapped, seriously emotionally disturbed, orthopedically impaired, other health impaired, deaf-blind, multi-handicapped, or as having specific learning disabilities, who because of those impairments need special education and related services."[13] Funding for special services is tied to a deficit model. If a child is not labeled defective and assigned one of the statutory labels, funding for supplementary services is not available, even though the child may have educational needs. Psychometric tests are required primarily because of the intricate "diagnostic" process which involves utilizing the pattern of scores on psychometric measures to pinpoint the nature of the supposed defect in the student. Children with specific patterns of scores are "diagnosed" as *having* a particular impairment—mental retardation, learning disability, emotional disturbance, and so forth.

When developing an educational program, it is the unique configuration of the child's needs, not the label, that guides program development. If funding were based simply on educational need, edumetric tests would suffice to identify the needy. It is questionable whether the naming game required by federal statute enhances educational opportunities for most children. In schools with multiethnic populations, the process can become highly discriminatory because children from non-Anglo backgrounds are more likely to be labeled defective.[14]

Fourth, psychometric tests have been used to track students into differing educational programs which have curricula that lead to different educational outcomes and lifetime opportunities. The rationale for such segregation is that it is easier to teach students in homogeneous groups. However, there is no firm evidence in the research literature that students *learn* better in segregated settings, especially slower students who can benefit from contact with higher-achieving peers. The federal mandate now requires that handicapped students be served in the least restrictive environment and the courts have seriously questioned both tracking and the use of psychometric tests in assigning students to various tracks.[15]

Testing to Infer Student "Intelligence"

The most controversial purpose for which tests have been used is that of inferring a student's "intelligence" or "learning potential" or "innate ability" from a test score. The primary difficulty in using any test for this purpose is that all tests measure what a person has learned. No test can measure genetically inherited intellectual ability.[16] What a person learns depends upon the language and culture to which the person is exposed. There is no such thing as culture-free learning, nor is there such a thing as a culture-free test. Hence, a test score reflects a student's *knowledge* of the language and cultural materials in the test. Knowledge is dependent upon cultural exposure, motivation to learn, an intact organism, and acquired test-taking skills, as well as one's inherited "intelligence." A person's ignorance of the materials in the test, however, does not necessarily mean that the person cannot learn the materials (i.e., that the person is "stupid"). The crux of the controversy is the confusion of "ignorance" with "stupidity." Since "stupidity" is a subset of "ignorance," a student may be either "ignorant but not stupid" or "ignorant and stupid." The problem is to differentiate between the two. Traditional assessment has no mechanism for making such a distinction; hence, it has treated all students who score low on so-called tests of "intelligence" as being both ignorant and stupid. These erroneous inferences have resulted in labeling disproportionately large numbers of persons from minority groups "mentally retarded" and "intellectually subnormal."[17] In a recent court decision, such inferences are no longer permitted when assessing Black students in the state of California.[18]

At least two procedures may be used to assist educators in differentiating the student who is ignorant of the material in the test from the student who is probably mentally retarded. In the first procedure, schools can examine the student's adaptive behavior outside the school —in the family, the community, the peer group, and the neighborhood. If the student is learning the skills needed to cope intelligently with the nonacademic world, then s/he may be ignorant of the skills needed to succeed in school but is not mentally retarded. Educational programs should be designed on the assumption that the student is capable of learning when motivated to learn.

A second procedure is to compare the student's performance on the test with the performance of other students from the same sociocultural background who, presumably, have had similar opportunities to learn the materials in the test. If the student's knowledge of the material is about what would be expected for a person with a given exposure to the test materials, then it would be rated "normal." On the other hand, if a student has learned significantly less than others who have had similar opportunities, then the performance would be considered "subnormal." Conversely, in identifying the gifted, if a student's performance is outstanding when the amount of cultural exposure has been taken into account, it would be rated "gifted."

Two methods can be used to determine the appropriate "norm" for making such judgments. Historically, testmakers have developed local norms whenever groups being evaluated have not been members of the population on which the test was normed. Local norms entail selecting a sample from the appropriate group and testing these individuals to establish the norm. Such sampling procedures are expensive and cumbersome because it is necessary to select as many samples as there are identifiable sociocultural groupings. Another method which is less expensive and quite feasible is to select one large, heterogeneous sample of the ethnic group in question. Using family sociocultural characteristics as the independent variables and test score as the dependent variable, testmakers develop a set of multiple regression equations. With these equations, it is possible to identify precisely the sociocultural norm which is appropriate for each combination of sociocultural factors. The student's score can then be compared with the appropriate norm. Procedures for making such comparisons have been developed for Black, White, and Hispanic students.[19]

"Intelligence" is a construct. It is not a physical characteristic, such as height or weight. It is not a specific set of behaviors. It is a hypothetical trait of the person which is inferred from an assessment of learned behaviors. How does one validate a test which purports to measure a hypothetical construct? Predictive validity is not appropriate, since we are not attempting to predict any specific future performance. Consequently, we must rely upon construct validity, the extent to which a particular set of measurement procedures reflects the theoretical construct. The logical paradigm is relatively straightforward. If two persons have had equal opportunities to learn the materials in a test, have been equally motivated to learn the materials in a test, are equally familiar with taking tests, are equally free from emotional disturbances or fears that might interfere with test performance, and are equally free from sensory or motor disabilities, THEN significant differences in their test performance may be interpreted as reflecting differences in their "intelligence." IF *all things are not equal,* then NO inference can be made about differences in their "intelligence."

To be a valid basis for inferring differences in "intelligence," a measure must have normative validity, that is, the persons being compared must come from the same sociocultural population and must not differ in emotional or physical handicaps. It would not be appropriate to compare a child with a visual impairment to norms based on children with good vision. It would not be appropriate to compare the performance of a six-year-old child to norms based on ten-year-old children because the six-year-old would have had less opportunity to learn the material in the test. Traditionally, tests have controlled for age differences by having age-specific norms. They have not recognized that controlling for sociocultural differences is also necessary in a pluralistic society if a test is to have normative validity. A federal court has recently ruled that measures which purport to assess "intelligence" must have normative validity, that is, the average scores for persons from differing sociocultural backgrounds must be the same.[20]

102

CONCLUSION

Because we are moving to new frontiers in multiethnic education, it is not possible to say with precision how testing and assessment practices will differ from the monocultural education of the past. As multilingual and multicultural curricula are expanded, we can anticipate a great expansion in edumetric tests designed to guide the instructional process. Norm-referenced tests will no longer be used to measure academic progress, to evaluate educational programs, to evaluate teachers, to categorize students as defective for purposes of funding, nor to place students in limited educational programs. They may be used to provide supplementary educational services to students who have educational needs, but not in the context of a defect model. Inferences concerning a student's "intelligence" will be made only after careful assessment of adaptive behavior in nonacademic settings and evaluation of the student's performance relative to the appropriate normative group. Before adopting a test in a multiethnic school, educators will require information on its validity for the purposes for which it is being used. They will demand documentation that the test is not racially and culturally discriminatory. If the test is to be used for prediction, they will want evidence that the predictions are equally accurate for different ethnic groups. If the test is to be used for making inferences about "intelligence," they will demand evidence that the scores have normative validity.

REFERENCES

1. M. M. Gordon, *Assimilation in American Life: The Role of Race, Religion, and National Origins* (New York: Oxford University Press, 1964).

2. M. B. Katz, *Class, Bureaucracy, and Schools* (New York: Praeger, 1971).

3. A. Binet and T. Simon, "Sur la Nécessité d'Établir un Diagnostic Scientifique des États Inférieurs de l'Intelligence," *Année Psychologique* 11 (1905): 1–28.

4. Carlos E. Cortés, "The Societal Curriculum: Implications for Multiethnic Education," in *Education in the 80's: Multiethnic Education,* ed. James A. Banks (Washington, D.C.: National Education Association, 1981).

5. L. M. Terman and M. A. Merrill, *Measuring Intelligence: A Guide to the Administration of the New Revised Stanford-Binet Tests of Intelligence* (Boston, Mass.: Houghton Mifflin, 1937), p. 22.

6. Ibid., pp. 48–50.

7. L. J. Kamin, *The Science and Politics of IQ* (New York: John Wiley, 1974).

8. T. A. Cleary, L. G. Humphreys, S. A. Kendrick, and A. Wesman, "Educational Uses of Tests with Disadvantaged Students," *American Psychologist* 30 (1975): 15–41.

9. R. Carver, "Two Dimensions of Tests: Psychometric and Edumetric," *American Psychologist* 29, no. 7 (1974): 512–18.

10. Ibid.

11. J. R. Mercer and W. C. Brown, "Racial Differences in IQ: Fact or Artifact?" in *The Fallacy of IQ,* ed. Carl Senna (New York: Third Press, 1973).

12. Ibid.

13. *Federal Register,* Sec. 121a.5, Tuesday, August 23, 1977.

14. J. R. Mercer, *Labeling the Mentally Retarded* (Berkeley: University of California Press, 1973).

15. Hobson v. Hanson, U.S. Dist. Ct., District of Columbia. 269 F. Supp. 401 (D.D.C. 1967).

16. Cleary et al., "Educational Uses of Tests."

17. Mercer and Brown, "Racial Differences in IQ."

18. Larry P. et al., Plaintiffs v. Riles, Superintendent of Public Instruction for the State of California, et al., U.S. Dist. Ct. for No. Dist. of Calif., before the Honorable Robert F. Peckham, Chief Judge, No. C-71-2270-RFP.

19. J. R. Mercer, *System of Multicultural Pluralistic Assessment (SOMPA) Technical Manual* (New York: Psychological Corporation, 1979).

20. Larry P. v. Riles.

CHAPTER 10

The Multiethnic Curriculum: Goals and Characteristics

James A. Banks

GOALS OF THE MULTIETHNIC CURRICULUM

A key goal of the multiethnic curriculum is to provide students with cultural and ethnic alternatives and to reduce ethnic encapsulation. Individuals who only know, participate in, and see the world from their unique cultural and ethnic perspectives are denied important parts of the human experience and are culturally and ethnically encapsulated. The multiethnic curriculum helps students gain greater self-understanding by viewing themselves from the perspectives of other cultures.

Another important goal of the multiethnic curriculum is to help students develop *cross-cultural competency,* which consists of the skills, attitudes, and knowledge needed to function within the individual's own ethnic culture, the universal American culture, as well as within and across different ethnic cultures. We need to determine the *levels* of cross-cultural competency that are appropriate and practical for students to attain. I have developed a typology of cross-cultural behavior.[1] Consisting of four levels—each of which is a continuum—it is designed to facilitate the determination of appropriate objectives and curriculum experiences in cross-cultural education.

At Level 1 the individual experiences superficial and brief cross-cultural interactions. At Level 2 the individual begins to assimilate some of the symbols and characteristics of an "outside" ethnic group. At Level 3 the person is thoroughly bicultural, tricultural, or multicultural. And at Level 4 the individual is completely assimilated into the new ethnic culture, has become desocialized, and is alienated from his or her original ethnic culture.

Neither Level 1 nor Level 4 cross-cultural behavior should be a goal of the multiethnic curriculum. Level-1-type school experiences, however, such as Chinese New Year, *Cinco de Mayo* (the Fifth of May), and special Jewish celebrations, are very popular in the nation's schools. In many schools these kinds of isolated activities are the only experiences related to ethnic groups. If they are the students' only experiences within the school related to ethnic groups, student stereotypes and misconceptions may increase rather than decrease, because such special days and programs often highlight the "exotic" and stereotypic characteristics of ethnic groups. In addition, historically, a major goal of the public school has been to socialize ethnic youths into Level-4-type cross-cultural behavior; that is, to make ethnic youths such as Blacks, Chicanos, and Jews culturally identical to Anglo-Saxon Protestants in attitudes, values, beliefs, and behavior.

Levels 1 and 4 cross-cultural behaviors are therefore inappropriate goals for multiethnic education. The multiethnic curriculum should help students develop the skills, attitudes, and abilities needed to function between Levels 2 and 3 of the typology. It should help students function effectively within a range of cultural and ethnic groups. The goal should be to make students multiethnic, multicultural, and multilingual in their attitudes, values, and behaviors. However, we should not alienate students from their ethnic cultures or force them to experience self-alienation and desocialization. Ethnic youths should not be required to deny their ethnic identity, ethnic heritage, and family in order to attain school success. Human beings are quite capable of being bicultural and to some extent multicultural. Students should learn situational behavior so that they will be able to determine which behavior is appropriate for specific settings and cultural environments.

Another important goal of multiethnic education is to help students master important reading, writing, and computational skills. Multiethnic education assumes that multiethnic content can help students master important skills in these academic areas. Multiethnic readings and data, if taught effectively, can be highly motivating and meaningful. Students are more likely to master skills when the teacher uses content which deals with significant human issues, such as race and ethnicity within our society. Multiethnic literature can help students master important writing, listening, and other communication skills.[2] Data about ethnic settlement patterns in our cities, their immigrations and migrations, and vital statistics about ethnic groups can be used to help students learn essential mathematical skills and understandings. Beginning in the kindergarten and primary grades, many students have questions about skin color and race. The teacher can use science and physical anthropology concepts to help students answer these questions. Multiethnic content should thus become an integral part of the total school curriculum. It should not be limited to special units, days, and lessons. If it is studied only on special days and occasions, students are likely to conclude that ethnic groups and their cultures are not integral parts of American society.

CHARACTERISTICS OF THE MULTIETHNIC CURRICULUM

The Complex Nature of Ethnicity

The multiethnic curriculum should help students better understand the complex nature of ethnicity within modern American society.[3] Misconceptions are widespread among the public, teachers, and students. When many students think of an "ethnic group," they think of non-White groups such as Black Americans and Japanese-Americans. They therefore confuse an *ethnic* group with a *racial* group. Teachers can help students better understand the complex nature of ethnicity within our society by helping them distinguish several concepts that are often confused, such as *ethnic group, ethnicity, ethnic minority group, race,* and *culture.*

We may define an ethnic group as a group which has a unique ancestry, the members of which share a sense of peoplehood, and which has some distinguishing value orientations, behavioral patterns, and political and economic interests. An ethnic group also tends to view the world from perspectives that differ from those within other ethnic groups. This definition suggests that Anglo-Americans and Irish-Americans, as well as Italian-Americans, are members of ethnic groups. An ethnic minority group shares these characteristics with an ethnic group. It has some unique physical and/or cultural characteristics, however, which enable persons who belong to dominant ethnic groups to easily identify its members and thus treat them in a discriminatory way. An ethnic minority group is frequently politically and economically powerless within a society. Black Americans, Jewish-Americans, and Chinese-Americans are examples of ethnic minority groups.

Ethnicity is a concept used to describe an individual's psychological identity with his/her ethnic group.[4] While membership within a particular ethnic group is largely involuntary, ethnicity or psychological identification with an ethnic group usually involves a large degree of choice. Some Blacks, for example, identify strongly with their ethnic group, while others have a low degree of ethnic identification. This is also true of members of other ethnic groups, such as Jewish-Americans, Italian-Americans, and Japanese-Americans.

Race is a problematic concept because physical anthropologists have been unable to structure racial categories that are consistent and widely accepted. The concept of race is used to differentiate and classify various human subgroups on the basis of their biological characteristics. Culture "consists of the behavior patterns, symbols, institutions, values, and other human-made components of society. It is the unique achievement of a human group which distinguishes it from other groups. While cultures are in many ways similar, a particular culture constitutes a unique whole."[5]

The foregoing definitions of ethnic group, ethnicity, ethnic minority group, race, and culture enable us to make some useful statements about these concepts. The definition of ethnic group suggests that every American is to some degree ethnic. It is best, however, to view ethnic group and ethnicity as *continuous* rather than as *discrete* concepts. In other words, it is more fruitful to raise the question "To what extent is an individual or group ethnic?" rather than "Is the individual or group ethnic?" The first question suggests that ethnic group and ethnicity are continuous rather than discrete concepts; the second that they are "either/or," discrete variables.

Ethnic Group: A Multidimensional Concept

Ethnic group membership is a multidimensional concept whose separate variables can be identified, even though they are highly interrelated. I have isolated eight major variables which can be used to conceptualize, measure, and determine the level of ethnic behavior of individuals or groups and the levels of cross-cultural competency of individuals (see Table 1). These variables are as follows:

1. Languages and dialects

2. Nonverbal communications

3. Cultural elements (such as foods, art forms, dances, and literature)

4. Perspectives and world views

5. Behavioral styles and nuances

6. Ethnic values

TABLE 1
Matrix for Conceptualizing and Assessing Cross-Cultural Behavior

VARIABLES	UNDERSTANDINGS AND BEHAVIORS	LEVELS OF COMPETENCY
LANGUAGES AND DIALECTS	The ability to understand and interpret the dialect and/or languages within the ethnic culture	1 2 3 4 5 6 7 ←———→
	The ability to speak the dialects and/or languages within the ethnic culture	←———→
NONVERBAL COMMUNICA-TIONS	The ability to understand and accurately interpret the nonverbal communications within the ethnic group	←———→
	The ability to accurately communicate nonverbally within the ethnic group	←———→
CULTURAL ELEMENTS	A knowledge and appreciation of cultural elements within the ethnic group, such as food, art forms, music, dances, and literature	←———→
	The ability to share cultural elements of the ethnic group, such as foods, art forms, music, literature, and dances	←———→
PERSPECTIVES AND WORLD VIEWS	The ability to understand and interpret the perspectives and world views that are normative within the ethnic group	←———→
	The ability to view events and situations from the perspectives that are normative within the ethnic group	←———→
BEHAVIORAL STYLES AND NUANCES	The ability to understand and interpret behavioral styles and nuances that are normative within the ethnic group	←———→
	The ability to express behavioral styles and nuances that are normative within the ethnic group	←———→
ETHNIC VALUES	The ability to understand and interpret the values that are normative within the ethnic group	←———→

TABLE 1—*Continued*

MATRIX FOR CONCEPTUALIZING AND ASSESSING CROSS-CULTURAL BEHAVIOR

VARIABLES	UNDERSTANDINGS AND BEHAVIORS	LEVELS OF COMPETENCY
	The ability to behaviorally express values that are normative within the ethnic group	←——————→
METHODS OF REASONING AND VALIDATING KNOWLEDGE	The ability to understand the methods of reasoning and validating knowledge that are normative within the ethnic group	←——————→
	The ability to use methods of reasoning and validating knowledge that are normative within the ethnic group	←——————→
ETHNIC IDENTIFICATION	Identification with the ethnic group that is subtle and/or unconscious	←——————→
	Overt actions that show conscious identification with the ethnic group	←——————→

7. Methods of reasoning and validating knowledge

8. Ethnic identification.

Each of these variables can be conceptualized as existing on a continuum. Measurement techniques can be structured to determine the level of ethnic behavior and traits possessed by individuals. This multidimensional conceptualization of ethnic behavior can help students understand that a person may be highly ethnic linguistically but very assimilated in terms of her/his values and perspectives. In addition, it can help students better understand the complex nature of ethnicity in American life and enable curriculum specialists to design more academically sound multiethnic units and lessons. It can also help mitigate some of the pernicious misconceptions about ethnic groups that are pervasive within the schools and the larger society.

Multiethnic Perspectives

The multiethnic curriculum should help students view American society and history from diverse ethnic perspectives rather than primarily or exclusively from the points of view of Anglo-American historians and writers,[6] as most school courses are currently taught. Courses and experiences of the latter type are based on what I call the *Anglo-American Centric Model* or Model A (see Figure 1). Many school districts which have attempted to reform their curriculum to reflect ethnic diversity have moved from a Model A-type curriculum to Model B, the *Ethnic Additive Model*. In courses and experiences based on Model B, ethnic content is an additive to the major curriculum thrust, which remains Anglo-American-dominated. Asian-American Studies courses, Puerto Rican-American Studies courses, and special units on ethnic groups in the elementary grades are examples of Model B-types of curricular experiences.

In the multiethnic school, the curriculum reflects Model C, the *Multiethnic Model*. In courses and experiences based on this model, students study events and situations from several ethnic points of view. Anglo-American perspectives are only one group of several and are in no way superior or inferior to others. However, I view Model D-types of courses and programs *(Ethnonational)* as the ultimate goal of curriculum reform. In this model, students study events and situations from multiethnic and multinational perspectives and points of view. Since we live in a global society, students need to learn how to become effective citizens of the world community. This is unlikely to happen if they study historical and contemporary events and situations only or primarily from the perspectives of ethnic cultures within their own nation.

To illustrate, when studying a historical period, such as the colonial era in American history, in a course organized on the Multiethnic Model (Model C), the inquiry would not end when students viewed the thirteen English colonies in North America from the perspectives of Anglo-American historians, as is usually the case. Conceptualizing the colonial period as only the study of the English colonies is limiting and Anglocentric.

Long before the English colonists were successful in settling Jamestown, the Spaniards had established colonies in Florida and New Mexico. Also, during the colonial period the French established a colony in Louisiana. When they study the Spanish and French colonies in addition to the English colonies, students are able to see that the region which became the United States was highly multiethnic during this period. Not only were there many different European nationality groups in North America at the time, but there were many different groups of Indians as well as Blacks. To gain a full understanding of the period, students must view it from the perspectives of the English, Spanish, and French colonists, as well as from the points of view of the many different groups of Indians and Blacks. The era of colonization had very different meanings for the Pueblo Indians and the Spanish colonists. It

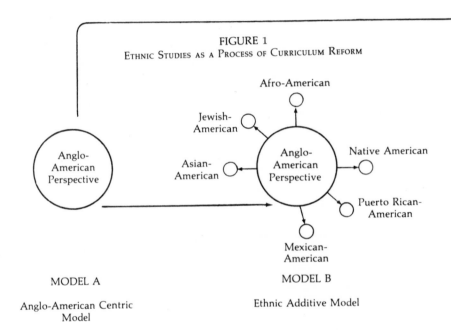

FIGURE 1

ETHNIC STUDIES AS A PROCESS OF CURRICULUM REFORM

MODEL A

Anglo-American Centric
Model

MODEL B

Ethnic Additive Model

Ethnic studies is conceptualized as a process of curriculum reform which can lead from a total Anglo-American perspective on our history and culture (MODEL A), to multiethnic perspectives as additives to the major curriculum thrust (MODEL B), to a completely multiethnic curriculum in which every historical and social event is viewed from the perspectives of different ethnic groups (MODEL C). In MODEL C the Anglo-American perspective is only one of several and is in no way superior or inferior to other ethnic perspectives. MODEL D, which is ethnonational, is the ultimate curriculum goal. In this curriculum model, students study historical and social events from ethnonational perspectives and points of view. Many schools that have attempted ethnic modification of the cur-

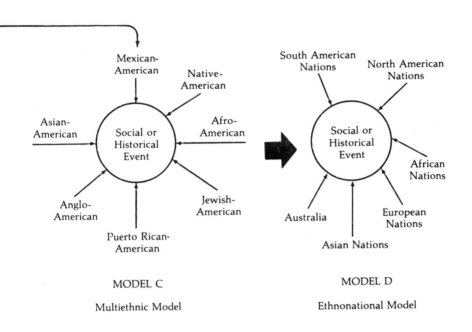

MODEL C

Multiethnic Model

MODEL D

Ethnonational Model

riculum have implemented MODEL B-types of programs. It is suggested here that curriculum reform move directly from MODEL A to MODEL C and ultimately to MODEL D. However, in those districts which have MODEL-B types of programs, it is suggested that they move from MODEL B to MODEL C, and eventually to MODEL-D types of curriculum organizations.

also had different meanings for the Black slaves, the free Blacks, and the English settlers. These diverse perspectives and points of view should be studied with a sound multiethnic curriculum.

I am not suggesting that we eliminate or denigrate Anglo-American perspectives on American society. I am merely suggesting that these perspectives should be among many different ethnic viewpoints taught in the schools. Only by teaching in this way will students gain a global rather than an ethnocentric and limited view of our nation's history and culture.

An Interdisciplinary-Conceptual Curriculum

Content related to ethnic diversity should permeate the entire curriculum; it should not be limited to the social studies, the humanities, or the language arts. Ethnic content is just as appropriate for such areas as home economics, physical education, science, mathematics, and art as it is for the social studies. Although it is often very challenging for the science or math teacher to integrate the curriculum with ethnic content, ethnic content can be incorporated into all subject areas. It is important that it be integrated into all subject areas so that students will be able to see how ethnic groups have influenced and contributed to American society in all walks of life and how each subject area can help us better understand the experiences of ethnic groups and consequently ourselves.

A conceptual approach will facilitate the implementation of a multiethnic curriculum which cuts across disciplinary boundaries. In this approach, the curriculum is organized around key concepts such as culture, socialization, power, and scarcity. Whenever possible, these concepts are viewed from the perspectives of such disciplines and areas as the various social sciences, art, music, literature, physical education, communication, the physical sciences, and mathematics.

Let's look at an example using the concept of culture. In reading and literature, students can read such novels as *Farewell to Manzanar, House Made of Dawn*, and *Bless Me Ultima*. They can determine what these novels reveal or do not reveal about the cultures of Japanese-Americans, American Indians, and Mexican-Americans. In drama, students can create a dramatization of the epic poem *I Am Joaquin* and discuss how it expresses Chicano history, contemporary life and culture. They can examine the works of ethnic artists such as Jacob Lawrence, Charles White, and Roberto Lebron in art. The language arts can focus on the various ways in which symbols and communication styles differ between and within ethnic groups and how American English is influenced by the ethnic cultures within the United States.

In science, students can examine the physical characteristics of the various ethnic groups and try to determine ways in which these traits influence the responses of other groups, group interactions, and their total culture. In mathematics, students can study the cultural roots of our base ten number system and discuss ways in which the number system within a society reflects its culture. They can also research the contributions which various ethnic groups have made to our number system.

Many excellent opportunities exist within the curriculum for teaching concepts from an interdisciplinary perspective. These opportunities should be fully explored and used. Interdisciplinary teaching, however, requires the wholehearted cooperation of teachers in the various content areas. Team teaching will often be necessary, especially at the high school level, to organize and implement interdisciplinary units and lessons.

MULTIETHNIC EDUCATION AND CURRICULUM REFORM

Changing the school to reflect the ethnic diversity within American society provides a tremendous opportunity to implement the kinds of significant curriculum reforms which are essential—including conceptual teaching, interdisciplinary approaches to the study of social issues, and value inquiry. Such change also provides opportunities for student involvement in social action and social participation activities. Thus, multiethnic education can serve as a vehicle for general and substantial educational reform. This is probably its greatest promise. We can best view multiethnic education as a process as well as a reform movement that will result in a new type of schooling presenting novel views of the American experience and helping students acquire the knowledge, skills, and commitments needed to make our nation and our world more responsive to the human condition.

REFERENCES

1. I first presented the typology of cross-cultural competency in James A. Banks, "Shaping the Future of Multicultural Education," *Journal of Negro Education* 48 (Summer 1979): 237–52.

2. Bibliographies of ethnic literature may be found in James A. Banks, *Teaching Strategies for Ethnic Studies,* 2d ed. (Boston: Allyn and Bacon, 1979).

3. This section is based on James A. Banks, "Developing Cross-Cultural Competency in the Social Studies," *Journal of Research and Development in Education* 13 (Winter 1980): 113–22.

4. Richard M. Burkey, *Ethnic and Racial Groups: The Dynamics of Dominance* (Menlo Park, Calif.: Cummings Publishing Co., 1978), p. 9.

5. Banks, *Teaching Strategies for Ethnic Studies,* pp. 56–57.

6. This section is based on James A. Banks, *Multiethnic Education: Practices and Promises* (Bloomington, Ind.: Phi Delta Kappa Educational Foundation, 1977).

CHAPTER 11

Multiethnic Education in Monocultural Schools*

Gary R. Howard

INTRODUCTION

Today, perhaps more than ever before, we as Americans are realizing how vast and volatile are our national and global differences in cultural, political, and religious commitments. Indeed, our survival as a nation and as a world depends more on our ability to deal positively with these human differences than on any other single factor. Given this awareness, what are we doing in our schools to help students become effective participants in a pluralistic world culture? Are we nurturing in them the knowledge and skills which will be necessary to bridge the chasms of ideology and emotion that separate the inhabitants of the planet and threaten our existence?

Learning to understand and deal positively with human differences is a theme which underlies multiethnic education programs across the nation. Few would argue that such a theme is an essential element of any comprehensive educational program. Yet this central thrust of multiethnic education has not been made available to the vast majority of

* The program discussed in this chapter has been developed as Project REACH (Rural Education and Cultural Heritage) in the Arlington School District, Arlington, Washington, under ESEA Title IV, Part C, funding.

students in our nation's schools, namely, those who attend schools serving predominantly White student populations.

The Ethnic Heritage Studies Act and other legal mandates and guidelines have had significant impact on large urban and racially mixed school districts, but have been essentially ignored in the rural, suburban, and other predominantly White school systems. There has been very little political pressure or economic incentive directing these schools to deal with ethnic diversity. Consequently, few programs have evolved. But where is the need greater? As Miel and Kiester have pointed out in their insightful study of culturally encapsulated White schools:

> In another period of history this sort of self-segregation might not have mattered. But today Americans cannot afford to shut themselves off from human differences, for these differences are precisely what the chief problems of our time are about.[1]

EDUCATION FOR DIVERSITY

It was this perspective that led us to design and implement a demonstration multiethnic education program in our relatively isolated and monoethnic school system in rural Washington State. With our student population 97 percent White and our professional staff 99 percent White, we felt we could make as good a case for cultural encapsulation as any other school system in the country. Given a 20 percent national and 80 percent global population that is non-White, we felt impelled to offer our students an educational experience which would prepare them for the realities of a pluralistic world. We simply could no longer afford to perpetuate an Anglo-centric perspective on U.S. and world history, and an Anglo-dominated notion of what it means to be a human being in the twentieth century.

Of course, this commitment to provide our students with multiethnic education was much easier to espouse than to implement. To realize our goal would require fundamental and far-reaching curricular changes. Furthermore, we would have to begin by laying the chief cornerstone of any effective change in curriculum—a sound professional retraining program.

THE REEDUCATION OF WHITE PROFESSIONALS

When we began to approach a multiethnic program in our monoethnic community, we had to first realize that most of the people on our professional staff, as well as in the community, had very little knowledge or personal experience with the history or culture of non-White ethnic groups. Some teachers had never engaged in a single relationship with a Black, Asian, Hispanic, or Native American person. We became aware that the students and teachers in some of our most affluent suburbs, as well as those in relatively isolated rural areas, are culturally deprived in the truest meaning of the term. They are unknowingly (or sometimes perhaps intentionally) denied access to the rich matrix of cultural and ethnic diversity which forms one of the greatest strengths of our nation.

The role of multiethnic education in Anglo-centric schools is to open up and broaden the world view of the participants in these schools, to enable students and professionals to become aware of just how unrepresentative and atypical their social reality is, and to encourage them to become actively engaged in learning about and learning from the many different cultural heritages that make up America. As Aragon has pointed out:

> We can't teach within a nation where cultural differences are extant if we don't know what the cultural differences are. Therein lies our dilemma. We can't teach what we don't know.[2]

Any attempt to reeducate White professionals for multiethnic education must proceed in a sensitive and gradual manner, with the trainers aware of the attitudinal and experiential background of the participants. From the perspective of Banks's typology of stages in the development of ethnic identity, most White Americans are extremely ethnocentric and encapsulated in a notion of the inherent superiority of the dominant White perspective on reality.[3] In the early phases of our training program, for example, one workshop participant commented that she wished we had more "minority" students in our school so we could use our newly gained knowledge to *help* them. In the course of discussion I reminded her that our entire program was designed to help *us*, not *them*. We as White people have too long denied ourselves an accurate understanding and a truthful perception of non-White peoples. Non-White ethnic groups may benefit from the increased awareness gained by Whites, but the primary beneficiaries of multiethnic education in the suburban and rural schools are the Whites themselves.

In the Arlington project we have found that teachers and administrators can move a long way in gaining a new multiethnic awareness if they are approached in a reasonable manner. We have found that it is not helpful to expend energy convincing teachers, administrators, parents, and students that they are White racists. Rather, we have adopted a nonconfrontive training process which provides valid, accurate information on the stereotypes, omissions, and distortions which are obvious in our Anglo-centric misdealings with the history and culture of all non-White peoples. Once exposed to this type of information, most clear-thinking people cannot help but perceive in their own terms the reality of racism. We have conceptualized our training program as a subtle, gradual attack on White ethnocentrism, a sensitive sabotage of our cultural isolation.

The training program itself proceeds in a series of three two-day workshops. Extensive utilization of non-White trainers allows cultural groups to "tell their own story" themselves rather than to be interpreted through White mouthpieces, which has so often been the case in the past. The process of White reeducation follows a three-phase model suggested by Grant and Melnich: Awareness, Appreciation, and Affirmation.[4] The Awareness phase involves self-awareness, human relations skills, and awareness of the role of racism in American society. The Appreciation phase emphasizes the transmittal of a vast amount of information about diverse non-White ethnic groups from a multidisciplinary perspective including historical, psychological, sociological, political, biological, linguistic, economic, and anthropological insights. The final phase of training, or Affirmation, engages educators in the actual work of developing a multiethnic curriculum for their particular school setting.

MULTIETHNIC CURRICULUM FOR MONOETHNIC SCHOOLS

The bottom line for any curriculum development program is its actual application in terms of activities and outcomes for students. Through our own trials and experimentation we have evolved a multiethnic/multicultural curriculum process that meets the needs of our predominantly White school setting. The process, which appears schematically in Figure 1, proceeds in four chronological phases:

1. *Human Relations Skills.* Any multiethnic program, whether in all-White schools, or in racially mixed schools, must begin with a strong emphasis on self-awareness, self-affirmation, and training in basic human relations skills. The goal of this phase is to create a supportive and trusting classroom atmosphere in which individual differences are acknowledged, shared, and valued.

2. *Cultural/Ethnic Self-Awareness.* In predominantly White schools it is normal for most students to feel a lack of cultural or ethnic identity. Therefore, before White students begin to study the history and culture of non-White ethnic groups, they must gain a practical understanding of the meaning of "culture" in their own lives. They

FIGURE 1. Four Phases in the Multicultural Curriculum Process

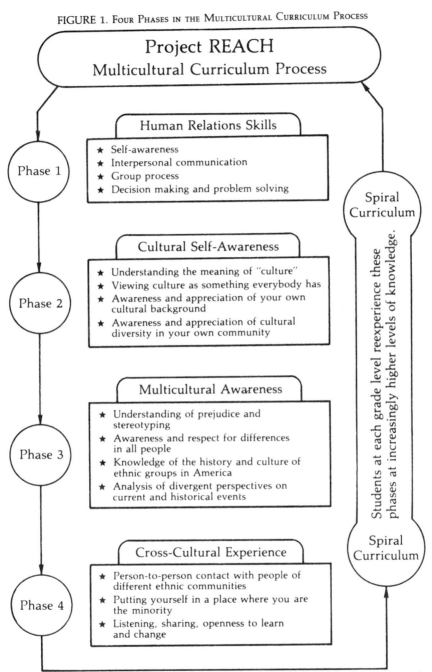

Project REACH
Multicultural Curriculum Process

Phase 1

Human Relations Skills
- ★ Self-awareness
- ★ Interpersonal communication
- ★ Group process
- ★ Decision making and problem solving

Phase 2

Cultural Self-Awareness
- ★ Understanding the meaning of "culture"
- ★ Viewing culture as something everybody has
- ★ Awareness and appreciation of your own cultural background
- ★ Awareness and appreciation of cultural diversity in your own community

Phase 3

Multicultural Awareness
- ★ Understanding of prejudice and stereotyping
- ★ Awareness and respect for differences in all people
- ★ Knowledge of the history and culture of ethnic groups in America
- ★ Analysis of divergent perspectives on current and historical events

Phase 4

Cross-Cultural Experience
- ★ Person-to-person contact with people of different ethnic communities
- ★ Putting yourself in a place where you are the minority
- ★ Listening, sharing, openness to learn and change

Spiral Curriculum

Students at each grade level reexperience these phases at increasingly higher levels of knowledge.

Spiral Curriculum

must realize that culture is something everybody has. For this reason we spend two months at the beginning of the school year guiding each eighth grade student in our American history classes in an exploration of his/her cultural background. Students construct a family tree, interview parents and nearby relatives, write letters to more distant relatives, and gradually piece together the story of their own cultural evolution. In this way the study of history becomes real for them and the concept of culture is appropriated in a personally meaningful way. Of course, we cannot force students to delve into their own family background, so they have the option of researching the culture and history of their hometown region, which ultimately meets the same objectives.

The culmination of this Cultural Self-Awareness phase is a Cultural Fair at which each student presents a visual display describing some aspect of his or her cultural story. Examples of project titles include German Foods and Recipes, Customs of Norwegian Christmas, Three Generations of Fur Trappers, Dairy Farming in Arlington, Irish Culture, Old Objects in My Family's Past, Logging Now and Then, and My Ancestor, Daniel Boone. The process of planning, creating, and displaying a cultural fair project fosters an appreciation and awareness of each student's cultural roots. It also provides an experiential insight into the great diversity of ethnic and cultural elements which exists, even in our "monoethnic" community. In addition, the fair allows for a positive expression on the part of those few students who do represent more diverse ethnic backgrounds, exemplified by project titles such as Spanish Fiesta, Japanese Culture in My Background, Judaism, The Trail of Tears, and Arts and Crafts of the Blackfoot Indians.

The Cultural Fair has become the highlight of our fall program, and broad community support and involvement have been generated over the past two years. It is a celebration of the history and culture of our community. Many families cooperate with their sons and daughters in the projects, and vast amounts of family folklore which might otherwise have been lost are discovered, renewed, and shared. We find it much easier to talk with our students about "culture" and "diversity" after the fair than before.

3. *Multicultural/Multiethnic Awareness.* The cultural fair process sets the stage for the next phase of the curriculum, the study of history and culture from the point of view of America's non-White ethnic groups. This phase requires a fundamental curricular shift away from an Anglo-centric perspective and toward a multiethnic ap-

proach to classroom content.[5] Rather than viewing events and concepts from a single point of view, that of Anglo-European ethnic groups in America, the entire curriculum is permeated with diverse ethnic perspectives.

For example, in our study of "Westward Expansion," we contrast the notion of the "Winning of the West," as viewed by the White settlers, with that of the "Losing of the West," as viewed by Native Americans. We balance our study of constitutional ideals and philosophy with a look at the system of Jim Crow laws which existed for years in direct contradiction to constitutional principles. Our study of World War II includes an analysis of the forced removal of Japanese-American citizens from their homes and lands, and their subsequent placement in concentration camps. A case study of the Mexican-American farmworkers and their perspective on the lettuce and grape boycotts is an integral part of our classroom approach to the growth of modern agriculture.

This multiethnic content is integrated into the classroom through the use of the *Project REACH Ethnic Perspectives Series,* a set of student booklets presenting American history from the point of view of non-White groups. Written with extensive input from non-White consultants, these booklets have proven to be stimulating reading material for secondary students. The goal of this phase of the REACH curriculum is that each student will be able to understand, to articulate, and it is hoped, to appreciate diverse ethnic perspectives on current and historical events.

4. *Cross-Cultural Experience.* To realize the goals of multiethnic education in predominantly White schools, the students themselves must be able to engage in significant person-to-person contact with people of different ethnic communities. In our program we have been able to provide this in a number of ways:

> *Guest Speakers.* Our students have enjoyed the presence of Black, Asian, Native American, and Mexican-American speakers in their classrooms. The mere fact that the students have an opportunity to interact with a sensitive and articulate adult from a non-White ethnic group helps replace a myriad of stereotypes with more accurate perceptions.
>
> *One-Day Field Trips.* We have taken our students to Mexican-American celebrations of Cinco de Mayo, on walking tours of Chinese- and Japanese-American communities, to Indian reservations to meet with tribal leaders and Indian students, and to Black theater productions at a nearby university.

Both careful and sensitive planning, involving the guidance of key people in the ethnic communities, and adequate advance preparation of students are imperative for these field trips.

Extended Field Trips. We have begun a tradition in our middle school of taking 15 to 20 students each year on a three-day field trip to a relatively isolated Indian village in the northwest corner of our state. In this way students gain the experience of being in the minority themselves, and of practicing the skills they have learned in the program for communicating effectively across possible ethnic barriers. Once again, meticulous planning and student preparation are crucial in making this an extremely effective learning experience.

Student Exchanges. Our experience has taught us that no single activity is more effective in creating positive attitudes than having our White students spend time getting to know young people of their own age, who represent diverse non-White ethnic groups. To provide this experience we developed an exchange relationship with an urban middle school with a 60 percent Black and Asian-American student population. Our teachers selected 30 students who they felt would contribute significantly to an exchange experience, and we took them to our "sister school" for a full day of attending classes and being hosted by a Black or Asian-American student sponsor. Although the students approached the experience with fear and trepidation, they returned enthusiastic about continuing the cultural interchange. The other half of the exchange was completed by having the urban students visit us. It is hoped that the relationship between our two schools will be institutionalized as a regular practice in the years to come. In this way we will continue to chisel away at the shell of our cultural encapsulation.

The entire curriculum model diagrammed in Figure 1 is conceptualized as continuous throughout the K–12 program. Students at each grade level can have significant learning experiences related to each of the four phases. Program reform will ultimately entail a complete integration of multiethnic content into as many aspects of the curriculum as possible. Because we want more than the mere addition of a few ethnic fringes to our dominant Anglo-centric curriculum, we are certain the process will take several years to implement fully. Our current developmental program has focused primarily at the middle school

124

level, but our overall professional training and curriculum development effort is K–12 in scope.

PROBLEMS, OBSTACLES, AND CAUTIONS

Although we are optimistic about the progress of Project REACH over the past two years, we do not want to be Pollyannas in our assessment of its overall impact. As anyone involved in multiethnic education knows, the problem of White racism is deeply rooted in American society, both institutionally and personally. Our best hope is for steady, gradual change, not instant panaceas. Some of the problems we have encountered include the following:

1. *Student Resistance.* A few students in our program have actively or passively resisted the information in the ethnic perspectives booklets or the participation in cross-cultural activities. In some cases we have been able to transform this resistance into positive discussion and growth, but in other instances it has been a holding operation at best.

2. *Parent Resistance.* We have had very little direct opposition, but occasionally parents will refuse permission for their child to take part in a field trip to a non-White community. In one case a parent was critical that multiethnic education was depriving his daughter of time spent in "basic education." For the most part, parents have seen the need for our program and actively supported each phase of the activities.

3. *Teacher Resistance.* Without exception, teachers who have participated in our training workshops have been positive and often enthusiastically active in their support of multiethnic education. In some cases, however, their support has been hampered by a sense of inadequacy or powerlessness to do anything meaningful in overcoming our legacy of racism. They have to be encouraged to take some small beginning steps toward changing their own curriculum and teaching style. Other teachers, not involved in the training program, have occasionally viewed our efforts with suspicion, lack of understanding, or perhaps as a threat to their own values.

4. *Anglo-Dominance.* A caution we must always keep in mind is that the multiethnic content in our curriculum is being delivered, for the most part, by Anglo teachers. There is a constant possibility of our falling into distortions, misappropriations, or lack of sensitivity to the actual experiences of non-White peoples. This reality necessi-

tates our inviting frequent review and critical comment from non-White ethnic consultants.

5. *Ethnic Exploitation.* There is a real danger of exploiting the few non-White ethnic individuals who live in a predominantly Anglo community. Teachers are sometimes tempted to use these students as examples or to make assumptions about a child's ethnic identity and self-awareness. Sometimes these non-White students will initially want to deemphasize or even deny their differences for survival purposes in a predominantly White environment. Thus far, all our non-White student participants have taken significant steps toward more pride and awareness of their cultural background, but this has been achieved through allowing them to grow at their own pace.

6. *Cautious Progress.* Multiethnic education is inherently threatening to any predominantly White school and community setting. It is a process which calls into question many of the basic assumptions and perceptions of Anglo America. For such a program to be successful, this element of threat must be acknowledged and dealt with sensitively. The professionals directing the multiethnic reform cannot be so confrontive as to run roughshod over the community's feelings, nor so passive as to avoid dealing with the realities of our history and racism. We have found that the best approach is to emphasize the positive outcomes for students through the cultural self-awareness and cross-cultural experiences. Although at times we feel we may be moving too cautiously and too slowly, our goal is to bring the community members along with us, rather than to leave them (and the program as well) in the dust.

7. *Dissemination.* One final concern is how to convince other predominantly White school districts to take on the multiethnic challenge. What is the incentive for them? How can the need be demonstrated? With all the multivaried demands made on educators today, how do we make a case for including multiethnic education in the "basic skills" program? How do we get in touch with and support those educators who want to move their predominantly White schools in a multiethnic direction?

CONCLUSION

The underlying goal of the Arlington experiment in multiethnic education has been to demonstrate the feasibility of developing a multiethnic program in a relatively monoethnic community. Although dedicated educators have been working for years to create effective multiethnic programs in urban areas with large concentrations of non-White ethnic students, the schools serving predominantly White student populations have for the most part failed to take their share of the responsibility. The students in these communities have an equal need and right to be provided with the knowledge, the skills, and the attitudes necessary for living effectively within a culturally pluralistic society. Our intention has been to achieve in our predominantly White school what the ASCD has determined to be "the essential goals of multiethnic education," namely:

1. Recognizing and prizing diversity,

2. Developing greater understanding of other cultural patterns,

3. Respecting individuals of all cultures, and

4. Developing positive and productive interaction among people and among experiences of diverse cultural groups.[6]

We are aware that we still have much to learn about how to implement such a program most effectively, but we have come far enough down the road to know that it can be done, and to invite other predominantly White schools to join us in the journey.

REFERENCES

1. Alice Miel and Edward Kiester, Jr., *The Shortchanged Children of Suburbia* (New York: Institute of Human Relations Press, American Jewish Committee, 1967).

2. John Aragon, "An Impediment to Cultural Pluralism: Culturally Deficient Educators Attempting to Teach Culturally Different Children," in *Cultural Pluralism in Education: A Mandate for Change,* eds. Madelon D. Stent, William R. Hazard, and Harry N. Rivlin (New York: Appleton-Century-Crofts, 1973), p. 78.

3. James A. Banks, "The Emerging Stages of Ethnicity: Implications for Staff Development," *Educational Leadership* 34 (December 1976): 190–93.

4. Carl A. Grant and Susan Melnich, "Education That Is Multicultural: A Model for Implementation Through Inservice Education," in *Curriculum Development and Inservice Education,* eds. Roy Edelfelt and E. Brooks Smith (Washington, D.C.: Association of Teacher Educators, 1976).

5. For an excellent analysis and schematic representation of stages in the development of multiethnic curriculum see chapter 10 in this book by James A. Banks.

6. ASCD Multicultural Education Commission, "Encouraging Multicultural Education," in *Multicultural Education: Commitments, Issues, and Applications,* ed. Carl A. Grant (Washington D.C.: Association for Supervision and Curriculum Development, 1977), p. 3.

CHAPTER 12

The Community and Multiethnic Education

Carl A. Grant

I have yet to meet the teacher who does not want to be successful in the classroom. By successful I mean helping students grow both academically and socially. In fact, most teachers acknowledge that their major rewards from teaching are directly tied to their classroom activities, particularly to facilitating students' success. Although student success directly corresponds to the teacher's sense of professional accomplishment, many teachers, especially in multiethnic communities, need to double their efforts to include a very valuable resource to help maximize student success in school. This valuable resource is the parents of the students and the members of the community.

The purposes of this chapter are to provide reasons for parent/community participation in schooling; to discuss constraints which hinder parent/community participation and suggest how these problems can be mitigated; to suggest ways of soliciting the help of parents and community members in schooling; and to describe the roles and contributions parents and community members can make to schooling.

REASONS FOR PARENT/COMMUNITY INVOLVEMENT

In many minority or multiethnic communities, the relationship between the school and the community needs major improvement. For example, besides the teaching of students, many school services to the community—graduation ceremonies, open houses, and sports events—are basically social. While these activities do bring in some community members, they usually involve only the parents of children who attend the school. Also , the parents are there merely as spectators because such events are neither designed nor planned to provide an opportunity for community input.[1] Even teacher-parent conferences may leave parents in a passive role if the teacher reports on classroom occurrences rather than solicits parent input. If parents and community members are frustrated by an inability to actively participate in school affairs, they may become alienated from the school instead of working out procedures for active collaboration. Let us examine some reasons for the need to actively involve the parents and the community in the schools.

Many social concerns, such as drug use among youth and a growing push to eliminate sexism, affect both the school and the home. Furthermore, the impetus for changes which affect the school has often come directly from concerned parents and community groups, sometimes in cooperation with teacher organizations. The movement toward legislation for educating all handicapped children within the least restrictive environment is an example. Given the number of social and educational concerns shared by both the school and the community, it is becoming increasingly important for teachers to actively work with parents and community groups. The extent to which this working relationship exists is more and more having an impact on what does or does not take place in the classroom. Even in the absence of an active working relationship, however, the community can often have a strong impact on the schools. For example, both the "back to basics" movement and the family-choice-of-schooling proposal (in California) were initiated by concerned parents and citizens without the involvement of teachers in the conceptualization and design of these plans. Because of mutual concerns and because the schools and the community frequently have an important impact on each other, teachers need to work more actively with parents and community groups.

The fact that the education of a person takes place both within and outside the school is another reason for active parent/community participation. Teachers need to work with and understand the students' home life and community in order to appreciate and "influence" the learning experiences of students outside the school. In fact, good teaching has to include not just classroom work, but also community involvement. A study that is presently under way is discovering that the majority of the teachers sampled do not have a general understanding of how and where students spend their time away from school, nor do they have a knowledge of resources available within the community.[2] Whereas teachers do not need to know their students' every move, it is important that they have a general understanding of student life outside school in order to better meet students' academic and social needs. Also, the knowledge and use of resources within the community may facilitate the development of more relevant and successful classroom academic and social experiences. An understanding of students' home life and community surroundings is critically important when teachers and students are from a different ethnic or socioeconomic group. For example, Teachers A and B were transferred to a newly integrated school. Both teachers were professionally competent and had a high regard for their students. Teacher B, however, scheduled out-of-school activities in order to learn about the home and community life of his students. This knowledge, he reported, enabled him to develop an excellent rapport with both students and parents. It also provided some of the understanding necessary to modify the ethnocentric curriculum in order to become more responsive to the needs and demands of his racially mixed classes. Teacher A did not take the time to get to know the community and the parents. Consequently, he felt out of place in his "new" school, and frustrated and professionally thwarted because he was unable to make the present teaching situation match the image of his previous one.

Parent/community involvement is also important because often, when visiting the school, parents will question the legitimacy and relevance of the educational program if learning is not taking place in a manner in which they were taught or with which they are familiar. Many worthwhile educational ideas have been impeded or stopped because parents and community members did not understand the concept, were not involved in the planning, and were not informed about the design and procedures. Teachers can facilitate understanding and acceptance of new ideas by informing parents about the proposed change and its rationale. For example, I know a teacher who wanted to change from a traditional to an open classroom. She consulted the parents and asked for their help in making the change in her classroom, explaining that she wanted to try a new method to "turn kids on." Not only did the parents recognize what the teacher was attempting to do, but they showed their appreciation by working with her.

School-community alliances are necessary because they can serve as the basis for helping students and community members critically analyze the circumstances of their lives. For example, teachers and parents/community members can discuss the conditions of poverty that pervade and control the lives of those of lower SES and many minorities.

They can share their understandings of the role of the school in relation to the student from a poverty-stricken background. Many minority and low-income people see the school as the key to better economic conditions for their children. Rather than viewing the financial environment of lower SES people as a debilitating factor almost impossible for schooling to redress, teachers can encourage this optimistic parental outlook. For example, during conversations with junior high teachers, I asked what they thought their students would be doing when they finished high school. Most teachers were skeptical about some students completing high school and described the greater number of their students as aspiring to and attaining only semiskilled or blue-collar jobs. Such expectations blocked these teachers from realizing that they may be dooming these students to the very prospects they described because of the lack of active encouragement to persuade them that they could rise above their impoverished circumstances.

The school cannot cure poverty, and it is not my intention to leave the reader with that conclusion. Teachers can, however, improve the school experience by motivating students to seek more schooling and/or to appreciate and strive within the schooling context. Teachers and parents/community people need to grapple with the way society is teaching students to think about their lives. Teachers and parents must teach students to challenge and fight the conditions which bind them to a cycle of poverty, and encourage them not to accept a fate they do not desire. Norms in school and society which enforce passive obedience must be addressed. While both teachers and parents/community people may agree that strict discipline is needed to promote learning, neither may realize that teaching strategies which place students in a passive, custodial role can have the effect of teaching them to passively accept the dictates of others and, thus, the economic conditions which dictate their lives. Through dialogue, these groups can come up with the kinds of experiences that can help students gain respect for the knowledge and analytical skills needed to address the powerlessness that pervades their lives.

Pointing out and emphasizing the power of the mastery of knowledge and skills for future opportunities is another "must." The wise teacher knows, however, that students will not grasp the significance of the power of knowledge unless that knowledge is interlaced with information relevant to their situation and taught by a teacher who they believe really cares about their future. Teacher expectations are important for this kind of teaching. Only when teachers perceive future opportunities for their students can they understand in what ways they may be able to influence them. In addition, teachers can help students develop a critical attitude by teaching them to question as well as to listen, to challenge as well as to accept.

Discipline is usually listed as the number one problem confronting teachers. Effective parent-teacher communication and cooperation can help eliminate minor discipline problems before they become serious. Also, an acquaintance with community leaders and a knowledge of community resources can provide teachers several avenues to travel in seeking solutions to the more serious discipline problems.

Finally, parent/community participation in the school can lead to better decisionmaking regarding the selection and allocation of school materials, goods, and services. For example, parents/community can influence personnel and policy decisions (such as the hiring of a bilingual teacher), the purchasing of materials to more appropriately respond to the backgrounds of students in the particular community, and the implementation of in-service programs to better enable the teacher to meet the academic and social needs of students. By involving the parents/community in such decisionmaking, teachers can benefit from their input.

BARRIERS TO PARENT/COMMUNITY PARTICIPATION

One constraint on parent/community participation is teacher anxiety. Many teachers are unsure of themselves when it comes to meeting and working with parents and community members, feeling as if they are on trial. This feeling is often compounded when teacher and parent are of different ethnic backgrounds. Teachers should realize that it is okay to feel anxious. Since the pre-service preparation of most teachers does not include experiences in parent/community-teacher participation, working with parents and community members is something that many teachers learn while doing.

The low pay of teachers relative to other professionals with the same amount of schooling (e.g., engineers), and society's negative attitude toward teachers can also operate as constraints on parent/community-teacher involvement. Some teachers believe that negative social attitudes toward them and the fact that many people assume that anybody can teach result in their receiving a lower salary than many other professionals. This belief may lead to less inclination to cultivate parent/community-teacher involvement.

A related constraint on parent/community participation is that many teachers do not realize that parents may be fearful of becoming involved in school activities because of their own unpleasant educational experiences. Many minority and low-income parents have few fond memories of the schooling process. For them school was a place of self-effacement and put-downs, where they were pushed out or dropped out. They may also think any blame for their children's unsuccessful school experiences will be placed upon their shoulders. For example, many minority and low-income parents think that teachers tend to believe that students' low academic achievement is directly related to family background; therefore, they avoid "facing" the teacher for fear that they may do something to support that belief.

Many minority parents—both of lower SES and middle-class—are reluctant to visit the school, especially to lodge legitimate complaints, such as the use of racially biased materials, because they believe that the teacher will take out his/her grievances on their children. Whereas we would hope that no teacher takes out his/her annoyance with a parent on the child, it is important that teachers realize that many minority parents do have these feelings and they may have to assure parents that such reactions will not occur.

Community members, especially those who do not have children attending school, may hold a negative view about education because a great portion of their property-tax dollars goes toward its support. Elderly people, in particular, need to be involved in school activities. They often feel that they are not getting "any return" on the money they have invested in the schools.

Another constraint on parent/community participation is the acting of community and school more from a posture of competition than of cooperation. With such a posture, both school and community are losers. Alex Molnar provides an illuminating comment:

> The argument over professional control versus community participation in curriculum decisions serves the interests of the dominant culture because it establishes a false and unproductive conflict. The conflict appears to be between professional expertise (which is claimed to be "objective" and value-free) and non-objective, value-laden interests of community members. Fundamentally, however, *the conflict is between the interests of those who want social relationships to remain as they are and those who would see them altered. The curriculum is the battleground but not the issue.*[3] (Emphasis added.)

He further notes, "In such battles, the interests of the status quo will always win if the problem or issue is not posed correctly and if the school and community stand apart from one another."[4]

SOLICITING PARENT/COMMUNITY PARTICIPATION

Obtaining parent/community participation is often a problem, even for teachers who actively promote the concept. Whereas it should be remembered that some approaches and techniques for cultivating parent/community participation are situational, the following suggestions have worked for a number of teachers.

1. At the beginning of the school year, systematically contact all parents or guardians of your new students by phone or in person, introduce yourself, and talk with them positively about the planned instructional program for the year and about your desire to have them participate in its implementation. But don't just tell them what is going to happen—talk with them and listen to them; solicit their views about what they would like to see happen.

2. Discover if home visits are welcome in your school community. If they are, make them to initiate parent/community assistance in the classroom, keeping in mind the following suggestions: make an appointment ahead of time; wear school clothes—don't overdress or underdress; keep your visit short—20 minutes to a half hour; avoid asking prying questions; and say something positive about the student.

3. Plan with parents to hold a parents' meeting during the first month of school at a time convenient for most parents. Discuss curriculum plans and governance procedures. Ask for assistance in several concrete ways to provide parents with the opportunity to become involved right away. Ask parents for topics they would like to see included in the curriculum.

4. Encourage parents to share with you the ways they have observed that their own children learn best. Ask them to encourage their children to bring to school projects that they are working on at home in order to share them with their classmates and to receive praise for their work.

5. Maintain a comfortable working classroom climate which demonstrates good management. Such a climate may directly influence the amount of classroom assistance and support you receive from parents and community members.

6. Introduce parents working in your classroom to the office staff, security guards, custodians, and any other persons they may encounter as they move about the building working with you. Not only will this introduction prevent the occurrence of embarrassing situations, it also says to the parents that you are proud of the relationship.

7. Improve teacher-parent rapport through school-home communication about positive things as well as about problems. For example, the Bailey Elementary School in East Lansing, Michigan, uses "Glad Notes" (postcards which pass along good news about students).[5] Some elementary and secondary teachers try to phone two parents every evening in order to contact each student's family regularly. If the number of students prohibits calling every parent, make an effort to contact the parents of students who would most benefit from the call. In addition, some school administrators place posters in local supermarkets and neighborhood stores announcing school events and methods for parent and community member participation.

8. If you are not bilingual and are planning to visit a student's home where English is not spoken by the parents, send a note home in the parents' language telling them of your lack of ability with their language but that you are still planning to make the visit. If the student can serve as interpreter, this will be a good opportunity for him/her to see the advantage of knowing two languages and to feel "important" by assisting two people who are very important in his/her life. If the student is unable to serve as interpreter, invite a trustworthy person to serve. Finally, make certain the parents do not feel "put down" because of their inability to speak your language.

9. Publicize school activities through organizations which play an active role in the community. For example, some high schools work with religious establishments to encourage community participation. Students who have demonstrated excellence in school performance (e.g., perfect attendance, good grades) receive public recognition during church services. School announcements related to the community are read at services or placed in church bulletins. This kind of cooperation between school and church has been very successful in low socioeconomic areas where the influence of the local clergy is very significant.

10. Become acquainted with the community itself, especially if you are not a resident. Read local newspapers and newsletters. Learn who the community leaders are and how they view the school. Discover what the major social and economic issues of the community are. Find out what the children do when they are not in school.

PARENT/COMMUNITY ROLES AND CONTRIBUTIONS

Parents/community members can contribute to schooling in two areas: at the specific level of a classroom and at the more general level of the school. The roles they may act out within the context of both the specific and the general levels vary widely, ranging from resource person in the classroom to member of the community council. The following discussion considers both areas.

Classroom Level

Parent/community participation in the classroom has a twofold reward: bringing parents to the classroom and involving them in actual educational experiences while creating a comfortable working relationship with the teachers and the school administration. In the past, many classrooms were places of isolation, where students interacted basically with only one adult—the teacher. Many teachers are diversifying their teaching practices, however, and certain educational innovations, such as the open classroom and learning centers, require assistance in the classroom to successfully meet their educational goals. Parents and other community residents can make a significant contribution in this area. Equally important, parents can serve as resource persons—guiding field trips and directing independent projects, for example.

In some high schools, parents or community members serve as homeroom advisers. Their responsibility is to be present during at least two meetings of the homeroom each month to help teacher and students with problems relating to attendance, job opportunities, personal careers, and school credits. Among other benefits, their participation enables the teacher to have individualized conferences with students in need of them.

Grandparents and/or senior citizens also can serve as resources to the classroom, providing information, skills, and experiences which broaden learning opportunities. They can recount personal memories, affording students a perspective on the past which expands and clarifies traditional historical reports. Invitations to parents and community people to share skills or information relating to current classroom activities allow students to see that knowledge comes from many sources and allow the teacher to make instruction more relevant to the students' backgrounds. Once an "open-door" relationship has been established between the home and the school, a variety of experiences can become available to enrich students' classroom learning with the additional resources of parents/community.

School Level

Parent/community participation at the school level may take several forms. For example, some schools (or school districts) have a parent/community advisory committee. This committee can serve as a forum where the concerns, wishes, and philosophies of parents/community, teachers, and school administration can be heard, and where these different groups can work together to give direction to the school program. Only recently (Opportunity Act, 1964, Title III) have parents/community members been actively encouraged to participate in school planning and decisionmaking. Title III, for example, states that federal grants may be made to local agencies, ". . . only if there is satisfactory assurance that, in the planning of that program or project there has been, and in the establishment and carrying out thereof there will be, participation of persons broadly representative of the cultural and educational resources of the area to be served."[6]

From the Teacher Corps, a federal program to improve the quality of education for low-income students, the role of Community Coordinator has been an important factor in improving home-school relations. Reliance upon the coordinator and community collaboration helps the project remain "true" to both the university-school and the community; it also helps the Teacher Corps interns learn and appreciate the dynamics of community participation in education. Schools, too, may benefit by learning from this Teacher Corps experience.

Some schools have established special-interest parent groups. These groups enable parents and community members to work in school activities in which they feel comfortable and have expertise. For example, parents/community members can head fund-raising projects for band equipment or serve as chairpersons on band trips. Parents are often pleased to be able to work with the school on short-term projects which provide the satisfaction of aiding student development and helping children successfully reach a goal. Participation also allows the parents to observe the direct benefit to their own children of school activities.

Serving as active members of the PTA or PTO is another way parents/community members participate in the activities of the school. For example, on a recent visit to a school in the East, I was informed by the principal that she needed more classroom space. Ironically, classroom space was available on an upper floor in the building, but the school administration was dragging its feet about releasing it. The PTO became aware of the problem and scheduled a meeting with the administrators, insisting that the administration give the space to the school or give a valid reason for not doing so. Within two days after the meeting, the space was released. Although it was said that this action was about to take place and that the meeting did not prompt the decision, parents acting together were very likely the deciding factor in accomplishing a great deal for the school.

The point here is that parents/community members can greatly influence the policies and procedures of the school. By working together to develop a spirit of camaraderie and cooperation, both home/community and school will benefit.

CONCLUSION

Finally, parent/community participation has changed since the militant sixties, when it was not unusual to have minority and low-income parents storming board of education meetings and actively demanding control of their schools. Currently, parent/community participation is carried out in a more peaceful atmosphere, as in community councils. The "peace" that presently exists will endure, however, only as long as schools continue to upgrade the quality of their performance involving the parents/community in their activities. "Although it is a delicate blend and requires tact and diplomacy, involving the people of a community [in the schools] has the potential of improving the lots of the people without destroying their links to their background and their conceptions of who they are."[7] This statement is especially true in minority and low-income communities where the history of schools has also been a history of racism, prejudice, and low expectations for the students.

REFERENCES

1. Carl A. Grant, "Partnership: A Proposal to Minimize the Practical Constraints on Community Participation in Education," in *Community Participation in Education*, ed. Carl A. Grant (Boston: Allyn and Bacon, 1979), p. 120.

2. Carl A. Grant, Lynn Boyle Ridgeway, and Christine E. Sleeter, *Students, Teachers, and Administrators in Their Workplace: An Ethnography of Educational Change* (Boston: Allyn and Bacon, forthcoming).

3. Alex Molnar, "Progressive School-Community Alliances as a Basis for Changing School Practices," in *Community Participation*, Grant, p. 250.

4. Ibid.

5. What Schools Are Doing, Public Relations, "Good News Notes: Painless Plan for Polishing PR," *Nation's Schools* 91 (March 1973): p. 40.

6. Elementary and Secondary Education Act, U.S. Code 20, sec. 844(a), 1970.

7. David Wiles and Houston Conley, "School Boards: Their Policy-Making Relevance" (Paper presented at the Annual Meeting of the National School Boards Association, Houston, Texas, April 1974).

CHAPTER 13

What Is "An Equal Chance" for Minority Children?*

Charles W. Cheng, Emily Brizendine, and Jeannie Oakes

INTRODUCTION

Any exploration of what comprises an equal chance for minority children must be made within the political, social, and economic context of society. An equal chance is, essentially, a culture-bound concept, defined relative to the dominant belief system and political and economic structures. In the examination of what comprises an equal chance for minority children in the United States, fundamental characteristics of American life must be carefully considered because of their impact on the definitions of equality and on educational reform efforts in that direction. Two underlying characteristics—the unequal distribution of economic rewards and the dominance of Anglo-American cultural patterns—are clearly linked in the educational arena.

First, this [chapter] will discuss the notion of an equal chance for American minority children by considering these two basic features and the changing conceptualizations of what comprises an equal chance. Second, commonly held schooling assumptions about the functions of education in the struggle toward equality will be examined. Third, an

* Reprinted with permission from *Journal of Negro Education* 48, no. 3 (Summer 1979): 267–87.

alternative paradigm for viewing the role of schooling in American society in relationship to the attainment of equality will be discussed. Finally, an argument for the full implementation of multicultural education will be made.

I. UNDERLYING CHARACTERISTICS

While equality has been the subject of endless public and scholarly debate in this country since the time of the American Revolution, implicit in American thinking has been the conviction that equality is a political entity, consisting of equal rights under the law. Tangential to this notion of political equality is the concept of individual competition for economic rewards. But, our economic and political structures are seemingly in conflict with the goal of equality of opportunity. Bowles and Gintis, for instance, indicate the contradiction between our political system and economic system. They observe:

> For the political system, the central problems of democracy are: insuring the maximal participation of the majority in decision-making; protecting minorities against the prejudices of the majority; and protecting the majority from any undue influence on the part of an unrepresentative minority. . . . For the economic system, these central problems are nearly exactly reversed. Making U.S. capitalism work involves: insuring the minimal participation in decision-making by the majority (the workers); protecting a single minority (capitalist and managers) against the wills of a majority; and subjecting the majority to the maximal influence of this single unrepresentative minority.[1]

This basic inequality and authoritarian character of the economic structure coexists with America's democratic ideology which emphasizes equal opportunity for all citizens. Even though this contradiction is a fundamental societal characteristic, the unequal distribution of economic power has not been viewed as inconsistent with the concept of equality. Economic distribution is seen as being based on meritorious achievement, rather than on ascribed characteristics, and competition is seen as fair. Thus, if schools can provide equal and fair competition, equality of economic opportunity is guaranteed. Accordingly, equal educational opportunity has emerged as the central ideology of American schooling. Since schooling has been considered the primary mechanism by which economic attainment is reached, public education has been a major focus for social reformers interested in providing an equal chance for minorities to participate in the "competition."

A second characteristic is the dominant impact of Anglo-American cultural patterns. For instance, historically, Anglo-American hegemony resulted in the assimilation expected of immigrant and minority groups. Although the United States has been a pluralistic society since its inception, the prevailing ideology has remained that of the Anglo-American majority.

William Greenbaum[2] suggests two overriding reasons why immigrant assimilation occurred so swiftly in this country:

> Most important is the fact that the main fuel for the American melting pot was *shame.* The immigrants were best instructed in how to repulse themselves; millions of people were taught to be ashamed of their own faces, their family names, their parents and grandparents, and their class patterns, histories and life outlooks. This shame had the incredible power to make us learn, especially when coupled with *hope,* the other main energy source for the melting pot—hope about becoming modern, and about being secure, about escaping the wars and depressions of the old country, and about being equal with the old Americans.[3]

As most immigrants quickly learned, adoption of Anglo norms, values, and behaviors was the unquestioned mode of participation in American social, political, and economic institutions. Similarly, minority groups have been largely influenced by this same socialization process. Both the dominant majority and most minorities, as Greenbaum noted, have been schooled to believe that conformity to Anglo-American cultural patterns is an essential part of being American. "Americanization" has been considered beneficial to the nation as a whole, in that it has provided a needed unifying element in society.[4] Likewise, "Americanization" benefits minority individuals because theoretically it provides them access to the Anglo-American "superior way of life." The popular rhetoric of the "melting pot" has only thinly disguised the fact that minorities, not the majority group, have been the ones expected to do the melting.

As would be expected, this assimilation pattern has had a tremendous impact on the struggle for an equal chance. Equality has been viewed only in the context of the Anglo-American culture. Schools have operated almost exclusively from the Anglo-American conformity perspective and reforms have, until very recently, left this aspect of the school culture unquestioned. A dominating belief is that the acquisition of the majority culture is a necessary means of gaining access to economic and political power. Significantly, the schools have been viewed as the place where minorities could acquire the essential knowledge, values, attitudes, and behaviors which would provide this access.

School reform efforts should be seen, in part, as a reflection of these dominant cultural beliefs.

An Equal Chance: A Changing Perspective

With the enactment of the Fourteenth Amendment to the U.S. Constitution, the notion of equality, or an "equal chance" for racial and ethnic minorities, was for the first time given legal sanction in American society. Historically it was hoped by the radical reconstructionists that an equal chance would mean full participation in American social, political, and economic life. The intent of the Fourteenth Amendment was undermined in large part by the Compromise of 1877; thus the hopes for equality by former slaves were dashed.[5] Not until the *Brown* (1954) decision would the Fourteenth Amendment be dramatically invoked to secure equal educational opportunity.

In the more than 100 years following the passage of the Fourteenth Amendment, the struggle to guarantee an equal chance for minorities has been primarily spearheaded by Black people and their organizations. Black political struggle has always been waged in the face of opposition from the executive, legislative, and judicial institutions at both the Federal and state levels. Even though large-scale political battles were being fought, education, as it was to the immigrants, was seen as the central vehicle for achieving an equal chance. For instance, the writings of such distinguished scholars as W. E. B. Du Bois and Carter G. Woodson emphasized the critical importance of educational attainment and advancement for Black people.[6]

As we all know, one of the first expressions of an equal educational chance took the form of separate but equal educational resources and facilities for Blacks comparable to those provided Whites. Fair competition being the premise of equality, it was believed that the provision of equivalent educational resources would equalize the competition between groups for future economic rewards. *Plessy* v. *Ferguson*, of course, functioned to accelerate the segregation of minority education, although as the overwhelming historical evidence suggests, equivalent facilities and resources were never a reality.

Although it was clear, early, that separate educational resources, did not result in political, economic, and social equality, it was not until the *Brown* decision that the legal view of an equal chance took a new form, that of equal access to the same educational resources and facilities. By 1954, it was widely believed that the separation of students by race, itself, had led to inequities in both resources available to students and the resulting achievement differences between racial groups. Indeed, the *Brown* decision underscored the importance of education as a cornerstone of democracy.[7]

With the *Brown* decision it was hoped that the speedy desegregation of schooling, by providing access to the same educational resources, would correct inequality. But the process of school desegregation alone did not result in equal educational achievement for members of different ethnic and racial groups. Here it seems pertinent to emphasize that throughout Black educational history various strategies—some recurring—have been invoked in attempting to achieve equal educational opportunity. Since *Brown*, integration and "community control" have been the most notable strategies. Yet, as Robert Newby and David Tyack point out, there has always been a common thread in these seemingly contradictory strategies—"most of the debates really concern the best strategies to achieve a common goal: power to Black people through schools that command equal resources and provide a quality of education that will enable the race to advance."[8]

About 10 years after the *Brown* decision, the now familiar research began to emerge demonstrating that desegregation of schooling, where it had been implemented, had done little to contribute to academic gains for minorities.[9] Desegregation had, at least in its first 20 years, failed to provide an equal chance at education and seemingly had little impact on problems related to economic inequality.

A new perspective of an equal chance developed in response to the disillusionment with the continuing inequality in educational outcomes in desegregated settings. While concerned with equal access to educational resources, this new perspective also considered equal performance as a critical variable. But equal educational performance was not possible if different groups of children did not begin schooling with equal conditions to do well. Thus, the cultural deficit hypothesis emerged to explain the continuing gap in minority and white achievement. Minority children were described as coming from disorganized and deteriorating homes and family structures. Such homes were seen as non-competitive and anti-intellectual environments which provided the minority child with little motivation for learning,[10] and little or no preparatory base for success in school. Central to this belief was the premise that school should eliminate so far as possible any of these barriers to the full development of individual intelligence. As a result, compensatory education to many meant "disadvantaged" individuals would be provided an equal chance to develop their particular level of intelligence.

In response, massive remedial, compensatory programs were

launched with the aim of changing the personal characteristics of these "culturally deprived" or "disadvantaged" students. Based on the assumptions that if these children could begin schooling equally, and those enrolled given a chance to "catch up," equal outcomes between groups would certainly follow. But, compensatory programs were basically designed to make the attitudes and behavior of minority and lower-class children more like those of the middle-class whites. The failure of these programs to achieve the desired equality has been widely documented.[11]

Compensatory education, of course, is founded on the thesis that the essential problem rests with the learner. Major political or ethical problems with the schools themselves or the people who administer and teach in them are not seriously considered by the deficit model approach. But many have questioned this underlying assumption. Ryan's succinctly stated criticism of compensatory education is typical of those who challenge the essence of the cultural deficit theory:

> We are dealing, it would seem, not so much with culturally deprived children as with culturally depriving schools. And the task to be accomplished is not to revise, and amend, and repair deficient children but to alter and transform the atmosphere and operations of the schools to which we commit these children. Only by changing the nature of the educational experience can we change the product.[12]

Failure of compensatory education programs to improve achievement in their target populations had, by the early 1970s, caused some thinkers to look in other directions for a means of equalizing the competition for educational attainment. Differences among students were no longer seen by some as the absence of necessary developmental experiences as a result of impoverished backgrounds. Reflective of anthropological theories of cultural relativity and linguistic theories of language and dialect competence, this perspective challenged the idea that providing children an equal chance meant eliminating cultural and ethnic differences. It must be noted, however, that this new emphasis did not supplant the generally held assumption of Anglo-conformity.

With this shift in thinking, the hypothesis of cultural difference replaced that of cultural deficit and changed, once again, the notion of what was necessary to insure an equal chance for minorities. This change directed the focus of some reformers away from the characteristics of the learners and toward the characteristics of the school experience as the objects of reform. The monocultural curriculum content, testing and grouping practices, and the expectations of educators for minority children came to be seen as the major barriers to educational equality. The structure and culture of the school, deeply rooted in the nation's Anglo-American conformity tradition, became the target for reformers with the move toward multicultural education as the means by which an equal chance could be guaranteed.

In the final section of this essay we will take up the underlying premises of education as multicultural and consider whether or not this approach can contribute to providing an equal chance. Here, we believe it appropriate to turn to a discussion of a few of the overriding schooling assumptions regarding equal educational opportunity for the minority child.

II. TRADITIONAL ASSUMPTIONS RE-EXAMINED

Three widely held beliefs assert that schooling and its expansion can provide equality of opportunity even in a society with large-scale inherent inequalities. It is the power of these beliefs which has prevented, until recently, a close examination of schooling and its relationship to the societal structure of inequality. Following our discussion of these three beliefs, we will consider an alternative perspective on schooling.

Meritocracy and Education

The first belief about the educational system is that the process is meritocratic in nature. Reflecting a dominant value orientation, this belief holds that status and success should be determined by effort, merit, and ability. Accordingly, achievement is deemed to be a more rational way of allocating status than inherited privilege. Past social reforms, including school reforms, have not infrequently been aimed at preserving fair competition needed for the emergence of an "aristocracy of individual talent."[13]

Equal educational opportunity, based on meritocracy, means insuring fair educational competition by removing social obstacles. In practice, governmental funding for compensatory educational programs reflects such an approach. From this perspective, educational opportunity focuses on individual responsibility. In effect, upon receiving extra compensation, the individual is expected to utilize available resources to compete fairly. Individuals not achieving success have only themselves to blame—lack of motivation or ability—since they did not avail themselves of the additional advantages made available by government intervention. Since the system is based on merit, the argument goes that those who rise to the top are the most talented and skilled. Those that succeed do so because they have the most drive, motivation, and academic talent. Essentially, this attitude reflects a belief in the fairness and neutrality of the educational process.

Recent critiques of schooling, however, have raised serious doubts regarding the relationship of educational achievement to economic reward. Even though school achievement appears to be determined by objective measures, test scores, and grades, Bowles and Gintis, for example, found a pattern of relationships between grades and certain personality traits, such as punctuality, dependability, and submissiveness to authority.[14] In this way, academic achievement is actually a measure of middle-class value conformity. Simply stated, schools are organized to reward certain values, and not others. Thus, the ideological neutrality of the school is questionable.

Studies indicating the effects of social origins on educational outcomes tend to further undermine the neutrality argument. Logically, the meritocratic thesis would seem to suggest that educational expansion will diminish the relationship between educational attainment (performance or persistence in school) and parents' social status. Nonetheless, Bowles and Gintis' review of available data indicates the number of years of school attained by children is as dependent upon family background today as it was fifty years ago. In addition, they found that neither the level of cognitive skills nor IQ can account for occupational attainment. Instead, a person's income was found to be dependent on his educational level and family status.[15] If meritocracy truly operates in the educational system, occupational status would have been shown to be a function of talent and motivation.

William Sewell summarized the cumulative disadvantages of low status students by stating, "We estimate that a higher SES student has about 2.5 times as much chance as a low SES student of continuing in some kind of post-high school education. He has an almost 4 to 1 advantage in access to college, a 6 to 1 advantage in college graduation, and a 9 to 1 advantage in graduate or professional education."[16] Thus, we believe there is persuasive evidence available at least to question the meritocratic thesis regarding public schooling.

Education and Upward Mobility

A second widespread belief which follows from the meritocratic thesis is that education provides an important avenue for upward mobility; therefore, expansion of equal educational opportunity enhances

147

the prospects for the talented and exceptional among the dispossessed —poor and minorities—to have a fair shot at high status jobs. Equalizing educational opportunities then is deemed as a positive means for affecting the distribution of material rewards in the larger society. As we pointed out above, belief in education is central to the American democratic ethos. Certainly, this belief has been bolstered by numerous studies which have documented that education is a key variable for occupational success or status attainment.[17] Nevertheless, two aspects related to the notion of the educational system as a vehicle for upward mobility require examination. The first is the expectation that educational expansion and increased access to educational credentials will lead to status mobility for minority groups. The second addresses the effects of this increased access: the actual translation of educational credentials into greater economic success and higher status for minorities. Both issues raise questions about the underlying assumptions concerning the role of schools in increasing economic and social equality.

As Greenbaum noted, hope can be seen as a pivotal element in examining the assimilation process experienced by immigrant groups in our earlier history. This is no less true today. Many of low socioeconomic status frequently cling to hope. Even though there is great despair in our ghettos, gilded ghettos, barrios, and reservations, the element of hope is not nonexistent among the dispossessed. Hope allows survival as people seek to cope with the unsettling life of the poor. Reformers, school officials, and concerned social scientists also hope that equal educational opportunity will lead to increased upward mobility for low status groups by providing the necessary educational credentials to succeed in the economic mainstream.

Educational expansion, it is believed, will equalize the distribution of the needed credentials. Yet, a consistent finding of research on occupational attainment is that when levels of educational credentials are equal, the socioeconomic status of parents is a strong predictor of the future status of the children.[18] In a 1967 study, for example, Blau and Duncan found that changes in rates of mobility over a period of time indicated that the relationship between the father's status and the son's status showed no consistent change between 1920 and 1960.[19] In other words, the ability to predict the occupational status of children from the knowledge of the parents' social status was just as great in 1960 as it was in 1920. Using data from the 1970 census, Blau and Duncan also confirmed the conclusion reached in their 1967 study, namely that the rates of mobility between nonmanual and manual occupations have not changed significantly in recent times.[20]

Significantly, these studies underscored the strong, consistent relationship of the parents' socioeconomic status and the children's occupational status or earnings. Thus, it cannot be necessarily assumed that the expansion of educational opportunity automatically leads to equalizing the distribution of credentials required for high status jobs. On the contrary, it would appear as though educational expansion has not reduced ability of high status parents to pass on their status to their children. Students from high status origins have consistently obtained more educational credentials than less privileged students. The gap between social classes in the acquisition of credentials needed for high status jobs has not narrowed. In sum, a number of studies examining educational achievement, social class, and social mobility provide no clear evidence that access to higher status jobs has been equalized. Yet, the persistent belief remains: low status groups will gain access to high status positions via schooling.

The "Model Minority" Myth. Although access to educational credentials has increased for low status groups, as the previous discussion indicates, translating this achievement into economic success remains debatable. In this section we believe it important to deal with one commonly held notion regarding the upward mobility of one particular minority group. Asian-Americans are frequently cited as being unusually successful in using education as a vehicle for upward mobility. In fact, Asian-Americans are often referred to as the "model minority."[21] This "model minority" image emerged because Asian-Americans have been able to achieve a higher level of education and greater upward mobility in comparison with other visible minority groups. However, in his examination of the "success" of Asian-Americans, Robert Suzuki found that while the group is one of the most highly educated ethnic groups in the country, education has not produced as much earning power for Asian males as it has for white males with the same educational background.[22] For example, his analysis of 1969 data from the U.S. Department of Labor, comparing the relative earnings of whites, blacks, and Chinese at different levels of education (high school graduate, college graduate, and postgraduate), disclosed that the percentage of Chinese males earning $10,000 or more was consistently below that of white males at the same educational levels, and below that of black males at the postgraduate level. Suzuki also examined data from the 1970 U.S. Census on median annual incomes of individuals, median years of schooling completed, and the median ages of whites, blacks, and three major Asian subgroups by sex. Again, he discovered that the median incomes of Chinese and Filipino males were only about 75 per cent of the median income of white males. While the median income of Japanese males was approximately 10 per cent above that of white males, Japanese males' median years of schooling and age were substantially greater than those of white males. Suzuki's findings led him to conclude that Asian-American males are generally "underemployed, underpaid or both . . . the celebration of their phenomenal 'success' as the model minority is at best premature, and at worst, a devious deception."[23]

Suzuki's analysis pointing out lower earning power for Asian-Americans even when they have attained an educational level comparable to whites would appear to contradict studies indicating that individual income is primarily dependent on educational level and family socioeconomic background. He suggests this earnings discrepancy for Asian-Americans is greatly influenced by stereotyping and racism.[24] Importantly, he also contends that the economic position of Asian-Americans may be affected by the differential socialization they receive in schools. It should be noted that while Asian-Americans have attained high levels of education, most of them have been channeled into white-collar jobs with little or no decision-making authority and low public contact. Suzuki believes that the limited upward mobility of Asian-Americans can be traced to the combined factors of a demand for workers to fill lower-echelon white-collar jobs due to an expanded economy after World War II, and the kind of socialization acquired by Asians at home and in schools.

In this instance, it seems appropriate to ask what role does schooling play for Asian-Americans. For us, Suzuki's observations, and those of others cited in this [chapter], indicate that in the case of Asian-Americans schooling is designed to maintain the unequal structure of American society by reinforcing and inculcating noncognitive traits in students which are characteristic of their family's socioeconomic background. Suzuki's preliminary analysis points out a need to examine in greater detail the treatment of cultural and ethnic factors in the process of schooling. While Suzuki's work is not definitive, this initial analysis does raise doubt about the belief in the educational system as a vehicle for upward mobility, particularly for minority groups. Clearly, before any substantive conclusions can be reached, more thorough research in this area is required.

Functionalism and Schooling

Failure of equalizing efforts through the educational system may be due to a third widely held view of the function and role of schooling. According to the traditional functional view, skill requirements in an industrial society steadily increase because of technological change. In such a society, education in complex industrial states serves to provide the specific skills and knowledge necessary for employment. Formal educational credentials signify that an individual possesses the skills and knowledge necessary for economic production. As technological changes create greater demand for highly skilled workers, educational requirements for jobs increase accordingly. An elite develops based on technological knowledge, and occupational stratification emerges. Occupational stratification is not dysfunctional to the system but is a necessary outcome because of the differing and complex technological needs of the society. Education, then, serves as a reasonable selection process. Since all in society have equal access to schooling, the completion of high levels of schooling and the resultant access to high status occupations are generally considered a matter of individual achievement. Understandably, the achievement model of mobility is followed where factors of ability and academic performance are held to be key determinants of career success.[25]

Recently, there has been much empirical evidence to dispute this functional notion of schools. Functionalists have been challenged by the credentialist school of thought. In part, credentialists share Max Weber's idea that society is composed of differing status groups competing for power. Credentialists maintain that members of all groups would like high status occupations and are capable of being trained for them. The school's function, say the credentialists, is not to train, but rather to teach people the cultures of different status groups.[26] Cognitive achievement and knowledge are not really important, because the level of educational attainment required for job entry in most occupations is far greater than necessary for efficient functioning on the job. Achieving higher levels of educational attainment, or "certification" becomes in and of itself the means of access to high status occupations. Furthermore, schooling discriminates on the basis of ascribed characteristics. High educational attainment and access to high status occupations and social position, therefore, is usually a result of belonging to a particular status group in society.

Not surprisingly, credentialists dispute the functional theorists' explanation of the relationship between educational attainment and occupational attainment. Ivar Berg has shown that there is little or no relationship between academic achievement and job productivity.[27] In addition, other evidence has suggested that educational credentials, rather than cognitive skills, are the best predictors of future status and earnings.[28] Collins, operating within the conflict model, has disputed the notion that the increase of educational requirements for jobs is purely the result of the demands of a highly technological society. For instance, Collins has indicated that employers have increasingly required higher educational attainment for even bottom-level jobs. There has not been a decisive shift, however, in the job skill requirements during the same time period as this increase in educational requirements. Within some jobs, educational requirements have outstripped needed skills. Thus, even though jobs have not changed, employers are demanding more education for those jobs. Collins concluded that education serves a credentialing function, with educational credentials being used to ration access to high status occupations.[29]

III. AN ALTERNATIVE PERSPECTIVE

Educational reform movements aimed at providing an equal chance for minority children have been largely based on the three predominating beliefs about the way schooling functions in American society discussed above. By not looking behind these assumptions, critical aspects of schooling which may have great impact on the role schools play in the attainment of equality have gone unquestioned. School reform movements have, for the most part, ignored the basic social, political, and economic context in which schooling takes place. Reforms and reformers frequently have ignored the powerful influence the form and content of the school experience itself have on those who attend schools. To be more precise, the following kinds of questions have been neglected: How has certain knowledge come to be more appropriate for school curriculum content than other knowledge? By what mechanisms have certain realms of knowledge been given higher status than others (science and math as opposed to vocational subjects, for example)? How have various types of school knowledge been distributed among groups? In short, we simply ask whose class and social interests have been served by the form and content of schools.[30]

Bowles and Gintis have suggested that school plays an important part in maintaining economic inequality among classes in American society. By socializing children differentially with the values and personality characteristics of the class of their origins, students are prepared to meet the demands of the occupations they will be expected to assume within the existing class structure. In addition, the educational process itself socializes students to accept as legitimate and inevitable the present social order and their future roles within it. In this way, schools as institutions function to reinforce the social relations of economic life. This is accomplished through "the close correspondence between the social relationships which govern personal interaction in the workplace and the social relationships of the educational system."[31] Bowles and

Gintis do not contend that the educational system operates in this manner as a result of the conscious intentions of teachers and school administrators, but rather as the effect of the close structural similarities in the social organizations of schools and the workplace. As the work of Bowles and Gintis suggests, through differential treatment of different groups of students the school actively reproduces the inequality of the larger society.

On the other hand, as Apple suggests, the school is not simply "a passive mirror but an active force, one that also serves to give legitimacy to the economic and social forms and ideologies so intimately connected to it."[32] Here the work of French sociologist Pierre Bourdieu is particularly instructive. Bourdieu, for instance, has analyzed the link between the dominant cultural values and the reproduction of economic inequality in a way that sheds light on American schooling reforms. Bourdieu contended that cultural capital, consisting of middle-class values, behaviors, and language patterns, is the commodity necessary for the acquisition of social and economic power in society.[33] Such an analysis seems consistent with the prevailing American belief that Anglo-American conformity is the central route to upward mobility. The schools, in Bourdieu's analysis, however, do not function to impart this cultural capital to those children who do not acquire it in their families. Instead, schools use cultural capital as a sorting mechanism for the distribution of children into their future societal roles. Schools function as though all children have equal access to cultural capital. However, we contend that cultural capital is unequally distributed as a result of the division of labor and power in society. By treating this cultural mode of the school as neutral (not serving the interests of any one group over others) and operating as though all children have equal access to it, the schools implicitly favor those who come to school having already acquired the linguistic and social competencies to function effectively in the middle-class culture. Compensatory education programs, assuming the neutrality of the system, attempted to change minority children by giving them more of the same. For example, more white middle-class culture and knowledge was emphasized, without ever questioning why it was considered the appropriate content of school knowledge, or the underlying function of a monocultural education system. We find Bourdieu's analysis instructive in helping to explain, as well, why multicultural educational programs are not universally implemented in our culturally pluralistic society.

In summary, we believe a critical analysis of the accepted beliefs about the nature of schooling—the belief in the neutrality and fairness of the educational system, the belief in education as a vehicle for upward mobility, and the belief in the functional purpose of education as one of imparting objective skills and knowledge necessary for a technologically complex society—contributes to an understanding of why school reform efforts have generally failed to increase equality in the society. Furthermore, the work of Apple, Bowles and Gintis, and Bourdieu suggest an alternative perspective on why an equal educational chance for minorities has not been achieved. Essentially, this alternative argument sets forth three main propositions: first, that American society is fundamentally unequal and this inequality is perpetuated by limiting the access of subordinate groups to political, economic, and social power; second, that the content and structure of schooling are not neutral, but actively reproduce this societal inequality through the knowledge and cultural mode which have been designated as high status and through mechanisms by which groups are sorted and treated differentially; and third, that schools are but a part of the larger societal dynamic which functions to perpetuate structural and cultural inequality. Seen from this perspective, it is clear that equality of educational opportunity emphasizing equal access cannot begin to provide an equal chance, in the fullest sense, to minority children.

IV. MULTICULTURAL EDUCATION—CONTRIBUTING TO EQUAL CHANCE?

Before considering whether multicultural education can enhance the equal chance of minority children in the context of the above discussion, a brief commentary on what we perceive multicultural education to be is appropriate.

The underlying premises of multicultural schooling are especially significant in that they conflict with the notion of the Anglo-American conformity. Proponents of multicultural education emphasize the effects that traditional ethnocentric schooling have had on minority children. Emphasizing Anglo-American conformity and middle-class culture, schools have expected minority children to understand and internalize the values, behavior, and culture of the majority. Such emphasis has resulted in minority children learning to reject their own cultures, history, and values. In contrast, the goals of multicultural education are to foster positive interactions among children of different cultural groups and provide educational experiences that are meaningful for all groups. Multicultural reforms recognize in positive ways the existing ethnic and cultural diversity of American society, emphasize an understanding of different cultural patterns, and nurture respect for the behaviors and values of different groups; and affirm the languages of cultural groups as being different, not deficient.[34] We also believe a multicultural school program should include a sociopolitical aim—to lead all individuals, regardless of their race or status, to acknowledge the right of all groups to exist culturally and to share status and power in American society.

With increasing emphasis on education that is multicultural, the perception of what constitutes an equal chance for minority children has shifted dramatically. Instead of merely stressing access to educational resources, the total educational program actively reflects a conviction that minority groups and minority cultural patterns are inherently equal. It follows, then, that efforts to impose a single cultural standard as a means of gaining access to social, economic, and political power are a violation of democratic ideals.

Due to the inequality which exists in society and our acceptance of the view that the seemingly neutral educational process is a "cause as well as an effect of the existing structure of social inequality,"[35] we are less than optimistic regarding the possible effects multicultural education will have on promoting an equal chance for minority children in American society. We share the viewpoint expressed by La Belle:

> Until a greater balance of socio-economic power is achieved among groups in this society, I do not believe that education for cultural pluralism is feasible. . . . [I]t is apparent to me that such a power balance will not be attained through the schools except as an adjunct to the distribution of resources like jobs, housing, political decision-making and the like in the wider society.[36]

Yet, we believe that the present monocultural mode of the educational system cannot serve as a democratic institution fostering anything akin to equal chance for diverse racial, cultural, and economic groups. Multicultural programs cannot, at this point, be assessed, as to their success or failure in providing an equal chance. Viewed in the context of basic American assumptions about the acceptability of economic inequality and the superiority of Anglo cultural patterns, it is no surprise that multicultural reforms have remained, for the most part, rhetoric.

We have suggested that multicultural programs have not been effectively integrated into instructional programming. A significant structural and political obstacle to the implementation of multicultural education is the fact that teachers are "encapsulated" within a social and economic context in which they and the schools are only a part. Apple has argued that "this very 'external' context provides substantial legitimation for the allocation of teachers' time and energies and for the kinds of cultural capital embodied in the school itself."[37]

When it comes to instructional practice, many multicultural programs have been little more than a recognition of ethnic heroes and holidays, or some inclusion of the contributions of ethnic groups in literature and social studies curriculum content. Such presentations of isolated information have little value outside the educational system because this knowledge is not considered part of the existing cultural capital. Even with the legitimacy of differences in the educational setting being affirmed by the *Lau* v. *Nichols* (414 U.S. 563, 1974) and *Wisconsin* v. *Yoder* (406 U.S. 206, 1972) court decisions, some consider multicultural programs and bilingual education as compensating for a cultural deficit (a first language or culture other than the dominant one) and only rarely as an integral part of the curriculum for all children.

Still, if multicultural programs could be implemented to the extent that their underlying goals were realized, multicultural education could possibly contribute in a significant way to furthering an equal chance for minorities in the larger society. As we indicated, one sociopolitical aim of multicultural education is the recognition by all individuals, regardless of race or status, of the right of different groups to exist and to have access to status and power in American society. To fully implement a program which attempts to achieve this goal, the movement must go beyond classrooms and toward effecting changes in the power relationships in the larger social, political, and economic systems. Should this occur, multicultural education could result in increased equality. Its major contribution would be its departure from the basic features of American society which shaped previous equalizing efforts. As indicated at the outset of this discussion, these two basic characteristics shaping reform efforts were the dominance of Anglo-American culture patterns and an acceptance of the inequalities of the American economic system.

Even though the obstacles to implementing multicultural programs are formidable, vigorous support for pluralistic schooling and the achievement of its goals should be continued. Even limited multicultural programs can be considered as valuable vehicles for bringing new knowledge to the existing school curriculum. Recognition of the intrinsic value of a diverse curriculum may improve the environment of the classroom and the quality of the day-to-day interactions of students and teachers.

Support of multicultural education, we believe, is essential in view of the promise it holds for expanding what is defined as the "valuable knowledge" imparted by schools. Multicultural education in school instruction may serve to erode the belief in the melting pot and the perpetuation of that myth. Clearly, the goals of multicultural education implicitly challenge the primacy of a dominant cultural value and perspective. Expanding the educational system to legitimately teach about other cultures and perspectives could be a modest attempt to challenge the dominant "common cultural currency."[38] An acceptance of the co-existence of several cultural perspectives may begin to erode a belief system which has been chiefly responsible for the inequalities in the political, economic, and social life of the country.

Despite our observation that we are not optimistic about school reform, we are fully cognizant of the contradictory nature of the American educational system. In spite of the role it plays in reproducing and justifying inequality, the educational system has not been a mechanistic reproduction institution, consciously manipulated by a dominant elite. As a result, schooling, as Bowles and Gintis note, has produced both "docile workers . . . and misfits and rebels."[39] With external contradictory and complex forces impinging on the educational system, multicultural education may serve in a small way to counteract the effects of the cultural and economic reproduction function of the schools. Contradictory characteristics of American education thus provide more than a ray of hope for us.

But we offer a final caveat. Unless there are some significant ideological shifts, we fear multicultural education could easily fit into prevailing pedagogical practices. Presently, the dominant schooling/pedagogical ideology promotes individualism, competitiveness, selfishness, and self-interest. Certainly, it is understandable why schooling in capitalist America would stress these particular values. Nonetheless, we would argue for another approach. We believe cooperation, altruism, caring and concern, and social responsibility *ought* to be the underpinning ideology for effective pedagogy in multicultural education programs. We agree with Elizabeth Cagan when she says: "There is an urgent need to structure groups purposefully so that cooperation and caring emerge because American youngsters are so heavily influenced by forces leading to individualism, competitiveness, and lack of social concern."[40]

Although one would expect that multicultural education would necessarily challenge these pervasive capitalistic/Anglo-American cultural values, it must be remembered that what we would characterize as *individualist ideology* is deeply imbedded in the fibre of the American national conscience, including American public school classrooms. Yet, hopes for a better society, we believe, rest on the possibility of creatively and responsibly working toward collectivism. Collectivism embraces social cooperation, social concern, and social responsibility. Schooling is but one place to begin. Cagan states the case exceptionally well:

> Adults have a responsibility for providing experiences that will encourage moral reasoning as well as moral concern, but this can be done only with an understanding of what is effective and why it is necessary. The basis for collectivist education is that we can use both the structure and the content of the educational experience to move children to an appreciation of the human bonds of sympathy and caring and that we can build a vision of a society in which these bonds can be realized.[41]

While we wish to move toward the realization of collectivist education, it needs to be underscored that those who see multicultural programs as a substantive strategy and collectivism as a guiding ideology must ultimately be concerned with providing an education that produces functional literates and critical thinkers. As Joseph Featherstone recently said, we need educators who are interested in children's minds.[42]

V. CONCLUSION

Finally, given the alternatives before us in dealing with the complex problems arising from the pluralistic reality of our society, the demand and support for education that is multicultural can be construed as basically a moral and an ethical issue. Despite the political, social, cultural, and institutional constraints on implementing multicultural education, a commitment to democracy provides no other alternative but one which promotes the respect for cultural differences, the increased participation of all groups in society, and, importantly, the eradication of glaring social and economic inequalities.

Our review here suggests that school reforms alone cannot do much to eliminate political and economic inequality. Nonetheless, intense efforts should still be waged to provide improved educational offerings. Our point is that we simply must be cognizant of the limitations school reform can have on correcting social injustices.[43] Efforts, however, to significantly improve the quality of schooling should be linked with a broader social movement concerned with struggling for and creating a more just society. Over 30 years ago, W. E. B. Du Bois, one of the most prolific and titanic scholars of this century, put it very concisely: "The demand of the twentieth century in America, just as the demand of the eighteenth and nineteenth centuries in Europe, is that the distribution of wealth be more logical and ethical."[44] When this occurs, we will have taken another step toward *insuring* an equal chance for those children now least served by public schooling in this country.

REFERENCES

1. Samuel Bowles and Herbert Gintis, *Schooling in Capitalist America* (New York: Basic Books, 1976), p. 34. While we are persuaded by the arguments made by Bowles and Gintis, we have found it instructive to review the equally convincing views of Michael Apple. Apple contends that Bowles and Gintis are too mechanical in their analysis. Several sound critiques have been made of the Bowles and Gintis thesis. See, David H. Kamen's review in *American Educational Research Journal*, 14 (Fall 1977), 499–510; and Randall Collins's critique in *Harvard Educational Review*, 46 (May 1976), 246–251.

2. William Greenbaum, "America in Search of a New Ideal: An Essay on the Rise of Pluralism," *Harvard Educational Review*, 44 (August, 1974), 430–431. Greenbaum's brilliant essay has considerably influenced our thinking. His essay takes into account significant Anglo-American cultural values often ignored by some revisionsists.

3. *Ibid.*, p. 431.

4. See, for example, William Greenbaum, *op. cit.*; John Higham, *Strangers in the Land: Patterns of American Nativism*, 1860–1925 (New York: Atheneum, 1963); David B. Tyack, *The One Best System* (Cambridge, Mass.: Harvard University Press, 1975), particularly Part V; Colin Greer, *The Great School Legend* (New York: Basic Books, 1972); Milton Gordon, *Assimilation in American Life* (New York: Oxford University Press, 1964).

5. See, Rayford W. Logan, *The Betrayal of the Negro* (New York: The Macmillan Company, 1954).

6. Each had a classic work on this particular subject. See, W. E. B. Du Bois, *The Souls of Black Folk* (New York: Crest Reprint, 1953); and, Carter G. Woodson, *Miseducation of the Negro* (Washington, D.C.: The Associate Publishers, 1933).

7. See Chief Justice Earl Warren's statements as cited in Alexander Kern, Ray Corns, and Walter McCann, *Public School Law* (St. Paul, Minn.: West Publishing Company, 1969), p. 643.

8. Robert G. Newby and David B. Tyack, "Victims Without Crimes: Some Historical Perspectives on Black Education," *Journal of Negro Education*, XL (Summer 1971), 193.

9. A wide body of literature has been written on this subject. See, for instance, James Coleman *et al.*, *Equality of Educational Opportunity* (Washington, D.C.: U.S. Office of Education, 1965); Christopher Jencks, *Inequality: A Reassessment of the Effects of Family and Schooling in America* (New York: Basic Books, 1972); R. P. O'Reilly (ed.), *Racial and Social Class Isolation in Public Schools: Implications for Educational Policy and Programs* (New York: Praeger, 1970); Nancy St. John, *School Desegregation: Outcomes for Children* (New York: Wiley, 1975).

10. See, Frank Riessman, *The Culturally Deprived Child* (New York: Harper and Row, 1962); and Nathan Glazer and Daniel Moynihan, *Beyond the Melting Pot* (Cambridge, Mass.: Massachusetts Institute of Technology Press, 1963).

11. H. A. Averch, *How Effective Is Schooling: A Critical Review and Synthesis of Findings* (Santa Monica, Calif.: RAND Corporation, 1972); Martin Carnoy, *Schooling in a Corporate Society* (New York: David McKay Company, 1972); and, Jencks, *op. cit.*

12. William Ryan, *Blaming the Victim* (New York: Vintage Books, 1972), p. 61.

13. For a brief but cogent discussion of equal opportunity from a sociological perspective, see, Philip Wexler, *The Sociology of Education* (Indianapolis: Bobbs and Merrill, 1976).

14. Bowles and Gintis, *op. cit.,* see Part II.

15. *Ibid.;* see Chapter 2 and Part II.

16. William Sewell, "Inequality of Opportunity for Higher Education," *American Sociological Review,* 36 (1971), 795.

17. See: William Sewell and Robert Hauser, *Education, Occupation, and Earnings* (New York: Academic Press, 1975).

18. *Ibid.*

19. Peter Blau and Otis Dudley Duncan, *The American Occupational Structure* (New York: Wiley, 1971).

20. Reported in Robert Hauser, "Temporal Change in Occupational Mobility and Evidence for Men in the U.S." *American Sociological Review,* 40 (June 1975), 279–297.

21. See, Harry L. Kitano and Stanley Sue, "The Model Minorities," *The Journal of Social Issues,* 29 (1973), 1–10.

22. Robert Suzuki, "Education and Socialization of Asian-Americans; A Revisionist Analysis of the 'Model Minority' Thesis," *Amerasia Journal,* 4 (1977), 23–52.

23. *Ibid.,* p. 41.

24. *Ibid.,* p. 42.

25. Carolyn Perrucci and Robert Perrucci, "Social Origins, Educational Contexts, and Career Mobility," *American Sociological Review,* 25 (1975), 451–463.

26. Randall Collins, "Functional and Conflict Theories of Educational Stratification," *American Sociological Review,* 36 (1971), 1002–1019.

27. Ivar Berg, *Education and Jobs: The Great Training Robbery* (New York: Praeger, 1970).

28. Christopher Hurn, *The Limits and Possibilities of Schooling* (Boston, Mass.: Allyn and Bacon, 1978).

29. Collins, *op. cit.*

30. Michael Apple, "Ideology, Reproduction, and Educational Reform," *Comparative Educational Review,* 22 (October, 1978), 367–387.

31. Bowles and Gintis, *op. cit.,* p. 12.

32. Apple, *op. cit.,* p. 386.

33. Pierre Bourdieu, "Cultural Reproduction and Social Reproduction," in Jerome Karabel and A. H. Halsey (eds.) *Power and Ideology in Education* (New York: Oxford University Press, 1977), pp. 487–510.

34. Carl Grant, "Anthropological Foundations of Education That Is Multicultural," in C. Grant (ed.), *Multicultural Education: Commitments, Issues, and Applications* (Washington, D. C.: Association of Supervision and Curriculum Development, 1977), p. 30.

35. Wexler, *op. cit.,* p. 24.

36. Thomas J. LaBelle, "The Rhetoric of Multicultural Education and the Reality of Schooling," in *Planning for Multicultural Education: A Workshop Report* (Los Angeles: University of California, L.A., Curriculum Inquiry Center, 1977), p. 77.

37. Michael Apple and Nancy King, "What Do Schools Really Teach," in G. Willis (ed.), *Qualitative Evaluation* (Berkeley, Calif.: McCutchan, 1977), pp. 444–465.

38. Randall Collins, "Some Comparative Principles of Educational Stratification," *Harvard Educational Review,* 47 (February 1977), 24.

39. Bowles and Gintis, *op. cit.,* p. 12.

40. Elizabeth Cagan, "Individualism, Collectivism, and Radical Educational Reform," *Harvard Educational Review,* 48 (May, 1978), 251.

41. *Ibid.,* p. 266.

42. Deborah Kops, "School Is a Window on American Life," *Harvard Magazine,* 81 (March–April, 1979), p. 85.

43. Henry Levin, "Educational Reform: Its Meaning," in Martin Carnoy and Henry Levin (eds.), *The Limits of Educational Reform* (New York: David McKay, Inc., 1976).

44. W. E. Burghardt Du Bois, *The World and Africa* (New York: International Publishers, 1976), p. 251.

CHAPTER 14

Teacher Preparation for a Pluralistic Society *
Walter Currie

At Trent University, I taught "Education and Native Peoples," a course that looked at the historical and contemporary relationships of the two while examining education in its broader context. During one phase of the course, we compared the cultures of Native and White children using various readings as the basis for our discussions. One reading, "The Environmental Factors in Socialization," gives the following comparison:

Native Child	White Child
Attitude Toward Child	
At age of mobility, child is considered a person and left relatively free to create and explore his own environment. He develops a sense	of independence and autonomy. Child is watched and controlled by parents and remains dependent on them throughout childhood.

---

* Reprinted with permission from the author and the National Dissemination and Assessment Center, California State University, Los Angeles, from *Cultural Issues in Education: A Book of Readings* (Los Angeles: National Dissemination and Assessment Center, California State University, 1978), pp. 38–48.

He has limited stimulation and feedback from adults.

He is not autonomous and has little opportunity to become independent.

pendent. He has constant interaction and feedback from adults around him.

Sanctions for Learning

Child is permitted to do things which interest him when he is ready. Seldom is he rewarded or punished for specific learning attempts although he receives approval when he does the task correctly after trial-and-error learning. Time is not a factor; he can take all morning to get dressed if he needs it. If child attempts a task and can't complete it, he is not urged to stay with it.

Child is urged to try things which are considered appropriate for him to know, whether he has expressed interest or not. He is rewarded for trying, whether he learns the task or not. Time is a factor: "See how fast you can dress yourself." Emphasis is placed on trying and on completing tasks undertaken.

(Hawthorn, 1967)

Eventually, during the seminar discussion, questions such as these were raised:

"How does a teacher cope with children in the same room when they are of opposite cultural backgrounds?"

"What does a teacher do if he/she is of a background similar to the White child but teaches only Native children?"

"Doesn't the methodology and standards of teaching, as presented at Teacher's College, relate mostly to the right-hand column child and not to the child in the left-hand column?"

This [chapter] attempts to answer these questions by examining the concept of pluralism, the determinants of school policy, the role of teachers, the child in a pluralistic society, teacher preparation, and some guidelines for teacher preparation to meet the needs of children in a pluralistic society.

PLURALISM

What name should be given to this "new acceptance" of the many cultures of peoples in North America? Should it be "biculturalism," "multiculturalism," "pluralism," "cultural pluralism," "cultural mosaic," or some other term? Banks (1976) discusses the differences among these terms and why they need to be clearly understood in order to ensure sound research to develop effective educational policies and programs. Concentration on "culture," he contends, could submerge the existence of "racism" as an issue relevant to the educational needs of children from various ethnic groups, instead of bringing both race and culture to the fore. He recommends that, "ethnic and racial diversity is a much better concept than cultural pluralism or multicultural education . . ." (p. 36).

One principal, when asked how many Indian children were registered, replied that he didn't know; such identification was unimportant since they "treated all children alike." And yet, the school register indicated which children were Indian as the basis for collecting school fees from the federal government. Dare "educational equality" be colour blind?

Before we resolve this issue, let us challenge the "melting pot" concept:

—The peoples of this continent are of many colours, races, creeds, and national origins, living all about us, especially in urban ghettos, barrios, and on the reserves.

—We live in numerous, differing geographical environments.

—We live in various political structures: nations, states/provinces, counties, reserves, cities.

—The motto, *E Pluribus Unum* (Out of Many, One), has included only those of the White race while excluding those whose skins are not white.

In 1971, Canada officially adopted a policy of "multiculturalism" as "a most suitable means of assuring the cultural freedom of Canadians" and "to break down discriminatory attitudes and cultural jealousies." Prime Minister Pierre Elliot Trudeau said further, "For although there are two official languages, there is no official culture, nor does any ethnic group take precedence over any other." Implicit in this statement is emphasis on the developing Canadian and on his developing culture and life style. This policy bridges the different cultural communities and the historically important English and French groups (Munro, 1975).

Many are concerned that this policy may result in a mere dress-up, song-and-dance time with some ethnic foods tossed in. The Canadian Consultative Council on Multiculturalism responded to this concern in its first report (1975) by warning against "truncated multiculturalism confined to such aspects as folk dancing, embroidery on women's clothing, decorative arts such as Easter egg painting, instrumental music, or even folk songs." In other words, multiculturalism is to constitute an integral part of everyday Canadian life; this implies *including incorporation of core elements into the educational process.*

In the same report, the Council raised the issue of ethnicity for its own sake, "Multiculturalism, [is] . . . the development of a consciousness of one's ancestral roots or ethnicity for creative purposes in the hope that a distinctive Canadian identity will emerge" (Munro, 1975). With regard to the latter, this writer, as a past member of that Council, recognizes the need for the Native peoples of North America to reaffirm and re-establish our ethnicity for our own sake, strength, and pride and, in turn, for "a [more] distinctive Canadian identity" and a more distinctive North American identity.

For one person's view of pluralism, let us turn to the Annual Report of the Ontario Advisory Council on Multiculturalism, where an Ojibwa mother is quoted: "As a child, my mother told me that when picking flowers in the woods to make a bouquet, don't just pick the most beautiful, have some of each kind of flower to make up the bouquet. This is the way I feel about the Canadian cultural mosaic." She speaks of a bouquet that is more beautiful because of the diversity of the flowers, all of which add to the total beauty, and yet, each is beautiful in its own right. It is within the diversity of this bouquet of peoples of North America that we must learn to live because in many significant ways we are alike, yet in many significant ways we are different. *It is the differences which must be recognized and accepted instead of being ignored or rejected.* A diversity of colours, languages, values, attitudes, foods, clothing, to name a few, characterize the people around us. From that diversity come the teachers of our children; of that diversity are our children.

THE DETERMINANTS OF SCHOOL POLICY

Society, with its diverse peoples, determines ". . . that the school reflects the values of the society it serves, values expressed not only by parental or community attitudes toward learning behaviour but also by governmental policy on taxation, on housing, on urban development, and [on] racial relations." The attitudes of minorities toward education cannot be disregarded by those who would teach or would suggest changes in education:

> *The Spanish speaking . . . often see themselves as the powerless victims of an educational system—run by a professional and political establishment which systematically excludes them from the process by which schools are governed, and from the decisions made about the education of their children.* (Valverde, 1976, p. 346)

American Indians have little, if any, influence or control in the education of their children in the public schools . . . (B) The white power structure often thwarts Indian attempts to gain representation on school boards . . . (D) A strong feeling of powerlessness pervades Indian communities in regard to their attempts to improve the education provided in public schools. ("Indian Education: A National Tragedy—A National Challenge," 1969, pp. 52–53)

Although there is diversity in the peoples who make up our society, there has not been diversity in the power structure which controls the education that all children are compelled to take.

According to Keppel (1969), ". . . we will have to accept the reality that changes in pedagogical tactics within the school's control have relatively little effect on social change or the creation of a new society. We, as educators, do not seem to have control over the important variables." If this is true, what recourse do schools and teachers have? Shall we bow to the inevitable and continue to develop "Pollyanna attitudes" in children who will face the same grim realities of dependency and powerlessness? In the preamble to the Code of Ethics of the National Education Association (1969), "We regard as essential . . . the protection of freedom to learn and to teach and the guarantee of equal educational opportunity for all." Are these mere words or do they have substance? If teachers, as Keppel's statement implies, serve as "change agents" only as directed, then teachers are only extensions and servants of the system, not co-determinants as befits a professionally responsible and respected group. Have we been misguided in believing that education is more powerful than it is? That, through education, society can be reordered? That social ills such as poverty, prejudice, unemployment, delinquency, and political corruption can be cured and prevented? That, through education, we will learn to behave in ways that respect everyone's present and future interests?

Can society change its expectations and demands of education to those which the system is capable of meeting? Or must we become revolutionaries, overthrow the system, and institute a new education? Illich (1971), for example, advocates "[creating] institutions which serve personal, creative, and autonomous interaction and the emergence of values which cannot be substantially controlled by technocrats."

THE ROLE OF TEACHERS

Is there "little social change or the creation of a new society" because potential teachers from that diverse society are actually exponents of the life style of the middle class? Future teachers are upwardly mobile, fearful for their jobs if they don't conform to traditional methods of preparing children for the "good life." Shepard (1968) asks,

". . . how many teachers, usually the very personification of middle-class values, virtues, and vices, are inadvertently condescending in their attitudes and interpersonal relations with the children they teach and with the parents of these children?" (p. 81)

Regardless of the quality of the curriculum—the textbooks, the courses of study, the school plant, the equipment, the administration—the effectiveness of an educational system is determined by its teachers because it is they who teach the courses of study and serve as identification models. They are obligated to meet the standards of reading and mathematics established by the policy makers. One could cite innumerable references to the failure of teachers and the system to deal successfully with children of a different colour, race, creed, culture, ethnicity, or socioeconomic status. According to a Senate report, "Teachers and administrators are often insensitive to Indian values and ignorant of Indian culture" ("Indian Education: A National Tragedy—A National Challenge," 1969, p. 53). In analyzing the factors contributing to low achievement levels of Indian students, the report cites ". . . the inadequacy of the instruction offered them for overcoming their severe environmental handicaps . . . the teachers . . . lack the training necessary to teach pupils with the linguistic and economic disadvantages of the Indian child successfully" ("Indian Education: A National Tragedy—A National Challenge," 1969, p. 62).

On the other hand,

In schools . . . highly approved by students, the teachers are well above average in their enthusiasm for teaching Indians, know more about the Indian community, have more contact with Indian students outside of school, rate higher on understanding and sympathy and show more favourable attitudes toward Indians than the average teachers . . ." (Fuchs, 1970)

How much of teacher ineffectiveness relates to the lack of successful models offered the culturally or racially different child? Grant uses the following statistics (from a 1975 report by the Department of Health, Education, and Welfare) to illustrate how schools have failed to recruit adequate numbers of minority-group teachers.

	Percent of School Population	
	Minority Students	Minority Teachers
Arizona	29.1	7.6
California	29.2	10.8
New Jersey	21.3	8.4
New York	26.6	5.6

In Native communities, local people are used in the schools primarily as caretakers, bus drivers, and teacher-aides.

THE CHILD IN A PLURALISTIC SOCIETY

We emphasize the importance of meeting the child's needs, becoming aware of individual differences, and understanding that no two children are alike. We emphasize the need for starting with the child where he/she is and moving from the known to the unknown. These are all familiar and accepted phrases. But, do we realize their implications for instruction?

From birth to age five, each child has learned much from his/her own explorations and his/her family. The child then undergoes a wider range of experiences among peers, relatives, and neighbours. Not only has the child learned to crawl, walk, and run, but to feed and dress himself/herself, speak a language, and begin to live by values and attitudes acquired by observing others. The child comes to school with a very complex store of previous learnings. But will the child find adequate opportunities to continue this learning?

For the child who finds school to be an extension of the lifestyle and culture of his home, learning will usually continue with few problems and every chance of success. But, if the Native child arrives at a school programmed for children from the White society, the Native child's learning will be directed to another cultural track beginning at 0.5 . . . , (as noted on the following graph).

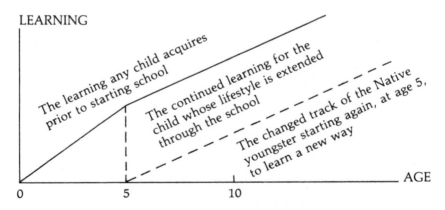

The child will receive a "Culture Shock," the full effects of which may not be identifiable for years. Students are required to learn another language and not use their own, to learn to be on time, recognize that tasks are measured by the clock, and to learn that almost everything is done differently in school than at home. The Native child has not continued to progress from his/her point of development, but has been

168

retarded by being moved to a suddenly new setting where all the rules are changed.

The culturally different child falls behind because he/she is "handicapped" by speaking a language other than English. The child's home and neighbourhood experiences have little relationship to those expected by the system because *the teacher is culturally unprepared.* Isn't it strange that the child at age six has to be ready to attend school, but the school does not have to be ready for the child?

TEACHER PREPARATION

Now let us look at the process of teacher preparation, a process that has been guilty, more by omission than commission, of perpetuating the myth of the "typical American" in curriculum. The depiction in children's textbooks and films of the dress, manners, customs, and family roles typical of the middle class has helped destroy those cultures which are different (Dickeman, 1973). This is the process to which the American Association of Colleges for Teacher Education addressed itself, when in May, 1970, a sub-committee recommended the establishment of a Commission on Multicultural Education to "Encourage member insitutions to include in their teacher education programs components aimed at the understanding of the multicultural nature of American life and the strengths of this diversity." In February, 1971, the newly created Commission submitted this resolution, ". . . That AACTE and its member institutions . . . establish as one of its top priorities provisions for multicultural education."

This resolution was followed in November, 1972, by the Commission's "Statement on Multicultural Education," which reads, ". . . schools and colleges must assure that their total educational process and educational content reflect a commitment to cultural pluralism . . . [T]eachers and personnel must be prepared in an environment where the commitment to multicultural education is evident." The Commission also suggested that there be ". . . faculty and staff of multi-ethnic and multiracial character, a student body . . . representative of the culturally diverse nature of the community, . . . and a culturally pluralistic curriculum that accurately represents the diverse multicultural nature of American society" (Hunter, 1974). If these enlightenments had come decades ago, there would not have been such statements as those of the Commissioner of Indian Affairs in 1887, "This language which is good enough for a white man or a black man ought to be good enough for the red man . . . [T]eaching an Indian

169

youth in his own barbarous dialect is a positive detriment to him. The impractability, if not impossibility, of civilizing the Indians of this country in any other tongue than our own would seem obvious" (Moquin and Van Doren, 1973, p. 110).

GUIDELINES FOR TEACHER PREPARATION IN A PLURALISTIC SOCIETY

First, as indicated previously, there are several needs that should be acted upon:

1. "Educational equality" means to accept each child as an individual.

2. Multiculturalism is a fact; the melting pot is an illusion.

3. Differences *and* similarities in children must be recognized and accepted.

4. "Schools" must do what they are capable of doing: helping young learners to think, not trying to cure society's ills.

5. Pluralism in society must be mirrored in the ranks of teachers.

6. The readiness of the school and of the teacher to receive the child as he/she is, is essential to the success of the child and of the educational programs.

Next, if the needs of children of "different cultures" and of "different races" are to be met; if the schools and colleges are committed to cultural pluralism; and if teachers are to be prepared to cope with their own "culture shock" for the benefit of all children, then what is to be done at the teacher preparation level?

1. Let those in teacher education practice what they preach, or at least make every effort to do so.

> a. If children are to be treated as individuals, why not the student-teacher? Professors should be expected to develop greater knowledge of, and contact with, individual teacher-education students. Since teachers are to care for their pupils, would it not be logical for the student-teacher to have experienced this "caring" to some degree in the teacher preparation courses at the universities?

> b. If the elementary school teacher is to work with a group of children over several hours and/or in various subject areas, why is this approach not illustrated in teacher education

programs? Why couldn't professors work together in teams? For example, there might be three professors and one practicing teacher from the field working with a group of students in teacher-preparation areas, covering a wide range of theory and *practice.*

c. Student-teachers are urged to use a variety of aides to help children learn; yet, professors lecture endlessly. The student-teacher is expected to stand before a class of children and communicate ideas verbally when that same student-teacher has been a passive learner with little opportunity to share in the planning of education courses or even to see the professor "practice what he preaches." In the book, *Schools and Equality,* the authors report that:

The most significant difference between personnel is that teachers in low SES schools have lower scores on a measure of verbal facility . . . [a] standard deviation [of] about 1.5 raw score points. (Guthrie *et al.,* 1971, p. 47) Are not most culturally different children—the Chicanos, the Blacks, the Indians, the Appalachian poor—in the low socio-economic schools? Do they not need good teachers?

d. Haubrich (1966) wrote, "One of these basic skills [lacking in teachers] is a fundamental knowledge of and an ability to begin a reading program within each classroom *no matter what the subject field"* (p. 366). Instead of blaming the classroom teacher, the press and the public should ask those at the teacher-preparation level why they aren't preparing teachers to help children learn to read.

e. In the Commission's statement concerning ". . . an environment where the commitment to multicultural education is evident," it is assumed that faculty involved in teacher preparation are also involved in the schools—consulting, supervising student-teachers, and conducting research. Their commitment to multiculturalism must be total if the student-teacher is to believe in the need for culturally and racially different children to have a chance.

2. Some guidelines for the teacher are: "a teacher tries to bridge the division between the races and to jettison the excess of time" (p. 29); "A Maori child should begin his reading from books of his own colour and culture" (p. 31); ". . . in judging Maori life . . . there is a Maori standard as well as a European one" (Ashton-Warner, 1963, p. 66).

In the following poem, Frances Brazil, of the Santa Fe Cultural School, captures the feelings of insecurity that often characterize the young Indian child.

Uncertain Admission

The sky looked down on me in aimless blues
The sun glares at me with a questioning light
The mountains tower over me with uncertain shadows
The trees sway in the bewildered breeze
The deer dance in perplexed rhythms
The ants crawl around me in untrusting circles
The birds soar above me with doubtful dips and dives
They all, in their own way, ask the question.
Who are you, who are you?
I have to admit to them, to myself,
I am an Indian

As Charnofsky (1971, p. 10) says, "There is growing evidence that the ability of children to be successful in our present American school system is predicated upon a healthy personal outlook and a relatively positive self-concept."

To be able to do those things Ashton-Warner suggests, to help children acquire a healthy personal outlook and a positive self-concept, and to counter the feelings of shame of being an Indian demands an atmosphere that says to the Native child, "It is good to be an Indian." To be able to create such an atmosphere for any child requires teachers to become self-critical of their own cultures and values. Through the behavioural sciences (anthropology, sociology, cultural psychology), through experiences with other races and other cultures, and through the development of communication skills, this awareness can be acquired. In turn, the teacher can better accept and appreciate the differences among human beings.

A girl of the Adawa tribe asked me a question which is the gist of this [chapter]: "Mr. Currie, can I get an education and still be an Adawa?" Does any sincere teacher dare answer anthing but "Yes"?

REFERENCES

Ashton-Warner, Sylvia. *Teacher.* New York: Simon and Schuster, 1963.

Banks, James A. "Cultural Pluralism and Contemporary Schools," *Integrated Education,* LXXIX (January–February, 1976), 32–36.

Carpenter, J. A., and J. V. Torney. *Beyond the Melting Pot to Cultural Pluralism.* U. S., Educational Resources Information Center, ERIC Document ED 115 618, 1973.

Charnofsky, Stanley. *Educating the Powerless.* Belmont: Wadsworth Publishing, 1971.

Dickeman, Mildred. "Teaching Cultural Pluralism," in *Teaching Ethnic Studies,* ed. James A. Banks. Washington: National Council for the Social Studies, 1973.

Fuchs, Estelle. "Curriculum for American Indian Youth," *The National Study of American Indian Education,* Office of Community Programs, III, No. 1. Minneapolis: University of Minnesota, 1970.

Gezi, Kalil L., and James Myers. *Teaching in American Culture.* New York: Holt, Rinehart and Winston, 1968.

Grant, Carl A. "Racism in Schools and Society," *Educational Leadership,* XXXIII (December, 1975), 184–188.

Guthrie, James W., George B. Kleindorfer, Henry M. Levin, and Robert T. Stout. *Schools and Inequality.* Cambridge: Massachusetts Institute of Technology Press, 1971.

Haubrich, Vernon F. "The Culturally Disadvantaged and Teacher Education, in *The Disadvantaged Child,* eds. J. Frost, and G. Hawkes. Boston: Houghton Mifflin Company, 1966, pp. 362–368.

Havighurst, Robert. "The Education of Indian Children and Youth," *Summary Report and Recommendations,* Office of Community Programs. Minneapolis: University of Minnesota, 1970.

Hawthorn, H. B., ed. *Indian Affairs and Northern Development.* Vol. 2, *A Survey of the Contemporary Indians of Canada.* Ottawa, Ontario, Canada, 1967.

Heron, John. "Canada's Adopted Citizens," *The Royal Bank of Canada Monthly Letter,* LIV, No. 11 (Montreal, Canada, 1973), 1–4.

Hunter, William A. "Antecedents to Development of and Emphasis on Multicultural Education," *Multicultural Education.* Washington: American Association of Colleges for Teacher Education, 1974.

Illich, Ivan. *Deschooling Society.* New York: Harper and Row, 1971.

"Indian Education: A National Tragedy—A National Challenge," *United States Senate Report,* No. 91-501. Washington: Government Printing Office, 1969.

Keppel, Francis. "Education and the Innovative Society," *Canadian Education Association Convention Proceedings.* Toronto, Ontario, Canada, 1969.

Mazon, M. Reyes. *Community, Home, Cultural Awareness and Language Training—A Design for Teacher Training in Multi-Cultural Education. A Program Outline for the Bilingual Cross-Cultural Specialist Credential.* U.S. Educational Resources Information Center, ERIC Document ED 115 588, 1974.

Michigan State University, East Lansing, Michigan, *Feasibility Study: Behavioral Science Teacher Education Program,* United States Department of Health, Education, and Welfare, Office of Education, Bureau of Research. Washington: Government Printing Office, December 31, 1969.

Moquin, Wayne, and Charles Van Doren, eds. *Great Documents in American Indian History.* New York: Frederick A. Praeger Publishers, 1973.

Munro, John, Minister Responsible for Multiculturalism, Ottawa, Canada. Address to Canada Iceland Centennial Conference (October, 1975) and Address to Ukrainian National Federation of Canada, Inc. (October, 1975).

National Education Association, Code of Ethics, Preamble, *Canadian Educational Association Convention Proceedings.* Toronto, Ontario, Canada, 1969.

Ontario Advisory Council on Multiculturalism, Annual Report, Provincial Secretary for Social Development. Toronto, Ontario, Canada, 1974.

Ontario Department of Education. *Curriculum Guidelines: Primary and Junior Divisions.* Toronto, Ontario, Canada, 1967.

——. *Curriculum Guidelines: Kindergarten.* Toronto, Ontario, Canada, 1966.

Shepard, Samuel, Jr. "The Disadvantaged Child," in *The Schoolhouse in the City,* ed. Alvin Toffler. New York: Frederick A. Praeger Publishers, 1968, pp. 77–85.

Sikes, M. P., and G. L. Coe. *Report on Teaching in Multi-Cultural/Multi-Ethnic Schools* (1974–1975). U.S. Educational Resources Information Center, ERIC Document ED 115 620, 1975.

Valverde, Leonard A. "Leadership Compatible with Multicultural Community Schools," *Educational Leadership,* XXXIII (February, 1976), 344–347.

Watkins, G. F., and D. G. Imig. *Utilizing Competency-Based Teacher Education as a Means for Facilitating Cultural Pluralism in American Schools.* U.S. Educational Resources Information Center, ERIC Document ED 115 613, 1974.

Wilcox, Preston. "Teacher Attitudes and Student Achievement," in *Education and the Urban Community,* eds. F. Hillson, Cordasco, and Purcell. New York: American Book Company, 1969.

Afterword

Multiethnic Education in the 80's: An Action Agenda

Eleanor Blumenberg

Early in 1975, against a background of revitalized ethnicity, a group of scholars gathered to discuss and debate pluralism in a democratic society, and its implications for the schools. The discussions were thoughtful, yet spirited; and the conflicting viewpoints covered a broad range of ideological, philosophical, political, and educational issues. Some conferees advocated a significant increase in multiethnic education on the grounds that it would enhance the reputation of minority groups in their own eyes and in the eyes of others, and generally enrich our national cultural fabric. Others expressed concern about adding new stereotypes to old, promoting social divisiveness, introducing artificial ethnic identities of doubtful value, and even decreasing the life chances of certain ethnic groups by interfering with the process of assimilation.[1] Terms like "ethnic studies," "multicultural or multiethnic curriculum," and "pluralistic education" were used interchangeably to convey differing but perhaps equally simplistic and loaded meanings.

The 1975 convocation mirrored similar confusion and controversy across the country. Agreeing only that melting pot notions were no longer valid and that education based on an Anglo-conformity model had failed large groups of American children, educational policymakers, often in response to outside pressures, instituted a wide variety of programs and policies. These included numerous federal, state, and local regulations; guidelines developed by professional organizations; separate ethnic studies courses, carefully isolated from the mainstream of instruction; textbook evaluations to determine their treatment of diversity; minority literature courses; bilingual education programs; the addition of ethnic heroes and holidays, feasts and festivals; and, only on rare occasions, a systematic renewal of a total curriculum and teacher preparation. Multiethnic education, in the 1970's, was a mile wide, but in most places, at best an inch deep.[2]

This present volume suggests that multiethnic education has come of age. Even the most casual reading of the preceding chapters reveals an evolving agreement on not only the imperatives of multiethnic education, but on its goals, methods, content, and conceptualization. While each author cogently addresses a special segment of the complex educational establishment, there is an underlying nonnegotiable assumption that multiethnic education is everybody's business and that the bits and pieces need to be systematically institutionalized into a coherent whole. As Geneva Gay puts it in her essay on classroom dynamics (see p. 52):

> Unless educators attend to the cultural factors—learning styles, value systems, relational patterns, and communication habits—which determine the environmental sets or climates of culturally pluralistic classrooms, other attempts to implement multiethnic education are likely to be minimized.

Similarly, focus on classroom alone without heeding what Carlos Cortés calls "the societal curriculum," or rules, regulations, reward systems, and labelling and sorting procedures, equally builds designs for failure. Nor can a vital program be developed without addressing the artificial dichotomy and unproductive argument between profession and community that Carl Grant has identified. Both segments are needed—from the highest policy levels to the smallest teaching units. In other words, if the promise and potential of multiethnic education are to be realized in the coming decade, an action agenda must involve all segments of the educational enterprise.

IMPLICATIONS FOR SCHOOL SYSTEMS

A recent roundup of school desegregation activity reveals that in at least the 3,000 school districts under court order or making application for federal funds to lessen racial isolation, some form of multiethnic or multicultural programming is taking place.[3] In addition, a great number of exemplary programs and materials are showcased at professional meetings or in journals. Much of this is laudatory, but it is safe to say that no single school district is programming systematically and continuously in all the areas that result in the incongruence between school and society so ably delineated earlier in this volume by Tomás A. Arciniega (see chapter 5). What then must be done?

Effecting meaningful changes in the schools' response to ethnic minorities requires the communication of a positive and overt affirmation of the "rightness and worth" of ethnic and cultural differences in children (see p. 54).

The following action agenda is indicated:

1. Clearcut articulation of policy that cuts across all levels, divisions, and individual responsibilities, and mandates infusion of pluralism throughout the system

2. Abandonment of additive and compensatory programs based on a deficit model

3. Study of staffing and school assignment patterns to determine how they might better reinforce appreciation of diversity

4. Confrontation with the allocation and delivery systems of the district (including testing and counseling programs) to see how these impact on multiethnic education

5. Development of new patterns of access and participation in terms of both student and community involvement

6. Provision of staff development, instructional materials, and individual support systems that facilitate the actual delivery of multicultural education to students.

To do all this, school systems can learn much from one another through exchanges of policy statements, curriculum guides, and instructional materials. Numbers of these are available from communities of diverse size, including Los Angeles, Buffalo, Minneapolis, Milwaukee, Cleveland, Denver, Seattle, and San Mateo. State guides have been developed in Pennsylvania, California, Minnesota, and Florida. Elementary curriculum materials include the *Individual Differences* guide prepared for the Madison (Wisconsin) Public Schools, and San Diego City Schools' *US: A Cultural Mosaic* (both currently being distributed by the Anti-Defamation League).

Also useful are the various checklists and needs assessment instruments, currently available, which evaluate both institutional and individual needs. Excellent ones can be found in some of the publications listed in the bibliography of this volume, including the National Council for the Social Studies' *Curriculum Guidelines for Multiethnic Education,*

James A Banks's *Teaching Strategies for Ethnic Studies* (2d edition), Carlos E. Cortés's *Understanding You and Them: Tips for Teaching about Ethnicity,* and the California State Department of Education's *Guide for Multicultural Education: Content and Context.*

TEACHERS AND TEACHER TRAINING

As Gwendolyn C. Baker and others have pointed out, the teacher is a pivotal figure in multiethnic education, yet often he or she is woefully unprepared. Traditional teacher preparation programs have just begun to confront ethnicity, whether it be in terms of teaching modes or learning styles or language differences. (See, for documentation, the chapters by Cox and Ramírez, and Saville-Troike in this book.) Furthermore, many of the first responses to ethnicity in both pre-service and staff development programs were based on a compensatory model, with differences coming across clearly as deficits to be removed or covered over.

An encouraging omen for the future is a new standard for accreditation adopted by the National Council for Accreditation of Teacher Education, effective January 1, 1979. Developed by a study committee of the American Association of Colleges for Teacher Education, the standard mandates that provision be made for instruction in multicultural education in both general and professional studies components, and should be addressed in courses, seminars, directed readings, laboratory and clinical experiences, as well as in practica and other types of field experiences. Commendably, the standard suggests

> Multicultural education should include but not be limited to experiences which: (1) promote analytic and evaluative abilities to confront issues such as participatory democracy, racism, sexism, and the parity of power; (2) develop skills for values clarification including the manifest and latent transmission of values; (3) examine the diverse cultures and the implications for developing teaching strategies; and (4) examine linguistic variations and diverse learning styles as a basis for the development of appropriate teaching strategies.[4]

The implications of this standard for accreditation for teacher training institutions are great. Invested with all its power and potential, it is a mandate for renewal and revitalization, a movement toward a new breed of teacher and administrator, sensitized to pluralism in the broadest sense and wedded to the creative uses of diversity as a teaching-learning tool. To effectuate it, all education departments must look at the messages they send out; and a college of education must reach out into other academic departments and into the community for added sources of curriculum. Sociology, the humanities, ethnic studies, the social sciences, psychology, and the ethnic enclaves of the surrounding community all can provide multicultural education building blocks. It is truly a challenge for the 1980's.

At least one school of education has begun its quest in systematic fashion. Working with consultants from the Anti-Defamation League, a group of core faculty from the University of Nebraska at Omaha has undertaken the development of modules to infuse understanding of the dynamics of prejudice into ongoing instruction in such areas as vocational education, administration, and legal aspects. Other universities are building on insights gained in a series of conferences convened under the auspices of the American Association of Colleges for Teacher Education and its Ethnic Heritage Studies Project. For them, multiethnic teacher education is an idea whose time has come.

Educators currently in the field, however, still need understanding and skills development. To that end in-service staff development programs, task-oriented, should be a priority agenda item. Here, too, the NCATE standard can serve as a working rationale and springboard for action for school systems, community groups, and professional associations.

PROFESSIONAL AND COMMUNITY ORGANIZATIONS

Over the past ten or fifteen years, a growing number of professional educational associations and other organizations concerned about racial, religious, and ethnic pluralism have issued policy statements and various publications, as well as undertaken conferences and other activities, aimed at helping win over America's schools to multiethnic education. Among the most active have been the National Education Association, the Association for Supervision and Curriculum Development, the National Council for the Social Studies, the United Federation of Teachers, the Association for Childhood Education, and the Council on Interracial Books for Children.

Effective ethnic, human relations, and civil rights organizations include the American Jewish Committee and its Institute for Pluralism and Group Identity, the Anti-Defamation League of B'nai B'rith, the Japanese-American Citizens' League, the National Association for the Advancement of Colored People, the Polish-American Congress, the Southwest Council of La Raza, and the Urban League, to name but a few

179

of the vital groups whose insights and resources continue to be helpful to educators. And indeed surveys of ethnic heritage curriculum projects reveal a sizable amount of school/community/ethnic organization co-operation.[5]

But there is still a tremendous amount of unfinished business on this front. Most professional educational groups have not infused pluralism into their day-to-day workings. They have not internalized the many noteworthy policy statements, guidelines, and publications they have sponsored on multiethnic themes. It is still a cause for surprise when outreach goes beyond the usual networks to involve others in conferences such as the NCSS 1980 annual meeting, with the theme Education for Participation, or the NEA Eighteenth Annual Conference on Human and Civil Rights in Education, focusing on Desegregation/Integration. There is still a marked need for leadership of professional associations to move ethnicity from advisory or parallel structures into the mainstream of their ongoing agendas.

FEDERAL AND STATE ACTIVITY

Moving beyond earlier legislation which focused on equality of opportunity and social justice, in the 1970's Congress enacted measures which challenged the very functions of the schools and their values of Anglo conformity. Legislation included the Ethnic Heritage Act, which to the time of this writing has funded several hundred curriculum projects; Title VII of the Elementary and Secondary School Assistance Act providing for bilingual/bicultural education, and various training and curriculum modification programs attendant to school desegregation and the lessening of racial isolation. Networks of federal general assistance centers have been set up, for bilingual, race and national origin, desegregation, and sexist concerns.

In 1977 with passage of legislation in Connecticut and Minnesota, thirteen states had mandated bilingual instruction. In addition, at least 28 states have enacted provisions covering some aspects of multiethnic education, including textbook criteria, teacher certification requirements, and staff development programs. In three states (Florida, Minnesota, and Pennsylvania) resource centers have been set up to provide materials reflective of the state's diversity of populations. Four states (Iowa, Minnesota, Pennsylvania, and Wisconsin) have made human relations training a requirement for certification. Some 35 state departments of education—among them California, Massachussetts, and West Virginia—offer in-service courses in multicultural or ethnic studies.[6]

But, here again, implications for future activity are great. Concerned educators, working as individuals or in concert with professional and community organizations, must do several things. First, they must become familiar with the enabling and the prohibiting rules and regulations where they work, identify like-minded colleagues and community supporters, and then move forward. In some areas, there is need still for further policy statements. In others, the task is the translation of these policies into meaningful programs.

A prime target for the 80's should be the area in which visible ethnicity is minimal, and where there are "no problems." Currently most of the legislation, funding, and action is beamed at urban, minority-dominated school systems. A task for the future is finding "carrots and sticks" for isolated, insulated school systems whose disadvantage may be less apparent, yet can be equally devastating to the short-changed students therein.

CAUTIONS AND CONCLUSIONS

The quest for effective multiethnic education yields no ready, easy answers or magic formulas, partly because it is as much a process as a program, as much a means to the educational goals James A. Banks has identified, as it is an end. In fact, a model too hastily applied can set in motion as many ills as it proposes to cure, just as a "miracle drug" can trigger disturbing side effects.

As Cherry A. Banks comments in her helpful chapter on becoming an effective cross-cultural counselor, when overly focused on group norms and characteristics, one runs the risk of losing sight of the individual, thereby perceiving and presenting him/her in stereotypic fashion. Ethnic diversity within American society is in fact no greater than the diversity within each individual ethnic group. An authentic multiethnic curriculum confirms that fact, rather than contradicts it.

Such a curriculum must also avoid the errors of past either/or programs which stressed either our very real similarities or our equally real differences. Each approach had limited success at best; and they shared a common failing. They tended to back away from the critical point of encounter between groups, especially when minority confronted majority. Studying slavery, the Nazi Holocaust, the Japanese relocation, or the Trail of Tears only as they are ethnically specific gives the false impression that ethnic history unfolds in a vacuum. A similar challenge is dealing with social ills and problems of prejudice without conveying the illusion that there are no positive aspects to ethnicity.

Statistics gathered by the U.S. Commission on Civil Rights reveal that most of our nation's schools, urban or rural, are racially and ethnically isolated. Obviously, cross-cultural schooling cannot be counted on to break down racial barriers and produce what James A. Banks calls "cross-cultural competence." The number of children going to one-race schools has been increasing since 1968, and levels of segregation are higher than those experienced by immigrants to the United States during the period of greatest influx at the turn of the century.[7] Consequently, the need is greater for educative experiences that can break down the stereotypes and feelings of superiority/inferiority that can flourish in isolated settings.

In a society increasingly fragmented and beleaguered, in a world that becomes more interdependent each day, it may well be that the promotion of human understanding is the most pressing (and basic) of priorities for educators. By shattering once and for all the myth that there is one model American, multiethnic education can increase social cohesion and national unity, while increasing the access to opportunity and productivity of previously shortchanged children. The editor of this volume has suggested that it can serve as a vehicle for general educational reform. More important, it can serve to make our schools more responsive to the human condition—truly, an action agenda worthy of the decade ahead.

REFERENCES

1. Melvin M. Tumin and Walter Plotch, eds., *Pluralism in a Democratic Society* (New York: Praeger Publishers, 1977).

2. For a fuller description of the responses of educators in the 1970's, see Eleanor Blumenberg, "Responses to Racism: How Far Have We Come?" in *Racism and Sexism: Responding to the Challenge,* eds. Richard L. Simms and Gloria Contreras (Washington, D.C.: National Council for the Social Studies, 1980), pp. 23–43.

3. *Desegregation of the Nation's Public Schools: A Status Report* (Washington, D.C.: U.S. Commission on Civil Rights, February 1979), p. 17.

4. "Standards for Accreditation of Teacher Education" (Washington, D.C.: National Council for Accreditation of Teacher Education, adopted May, 1977, effective January 1, 1979).

5. Information about ethnic heritage studies curriculum projects and sample curricula are available from the Ethnic Heritage Clearinghouse, 855 Broadway, Boulder, CO 80302.

6. Raymond H. Giles and Donna M. Gollnick, "Ethnic/Cultural Diversity as Reflected in Federal and State Educational Legislation and Policies," in *Pluralism and the American Teacher,* eds. Frank H. Klassen and Donna M. Gollnick (Washington, D.C.: American Association of Colleges for Teacher Education, 1977), pp. 115–60.

7. *Desegregation of the Nation's Public Schools,* p. 20.

Multiethnic Education: Basic References

James A. Banks

Banks, James A.; Cortés, Carlos E.; Gay, Geneva; Garcia, Ricardo L.; and Ochoa, Anna S. *Curriculum Guidelines for Multiethnic Education*. Washington, D.C.: National Council for the Social Studies, 1976.

This NCSS position statement includes a rationale for ethnic pluralism, 23 guidelines for establishing effective multiethnic educational programs, and an evaluation checklist.

Banks, James A. *Multiethnic Education: Theory and Practice*. Boston: Allyn and Bacon, 1981.

This book discusses historical, conceptual, and philosophical issues in the fields of multiethnic and multicultural education. Among the other topics discussed are teaching strategies for multiethnic education, linking multiethnic and global education, and ethnicity and citizenship education.

Banks, James A. *Teaching Strategies for Ethnic Studies*. 2d ed. Boston: Allyn and Bacon, 1979.

Teaching strategies, with grade levels designated, and bibliographies for teachers and students are among the key features of this book. Also included are a historical overview and a chronology of key events for all major American ethnic groups. The book is designed as a sourcebook for classroom teachers as well as a text for courses in ethnic studies and in multicultural education.

Baptiste, H. Prentice, Jr. *Multicultural Education: A Synopsis*. Washington, D.C.: University Press of America, 1976.

This monograph includes a discussion of definitions, models, and issues related to multicultural education.

Cortés, Carlos E., with Fay Metcalf and Sharryl Hawke. *Understanding You and Them: Tips for Teaching About Ethnicity*. Boulder: Social Science Education Consortium, 1976.

Cortés's essay, "Ethnicity in the Curriculum," is provocative and useful. The book also includes a set of teaching activities and helpful information about evaluating the multiethnic curriculum.

Cross, Dolores E.; Baker, Gwendolyn; and Stiles, Lindley J., eds. *Teaching in a Multicultural Society: Perspectives and Professional Strategies.* New York: Macmillan, 1977.

The contributors to this book, who include Meyer Weinberg, James Deslonde, and Asa Hilliard, focus on ways of changing the school curriculum to reflect the ethnic and cultural diversity in American society.

Garcia, Ricardo L. *Learning in Two Languages.* Bloomington, Ind.: Phi Delta Kappa Educational Foundation, 1976.

This booklet explores the importance and implications of bilingual education and is available in English and Spanish editions.

Gold, Milton J.; Grant, Carl A.; and Rivlin, Harry N.; eds. *In Praise of Diversity: A Resource Book for Multicultural Education.* Washington, D.C.: Association of Teacher Educators, 1977.

This volume contains several interesting and informative historical overviews of various ethnic groups. Geneva Gay, Richard Gambino, and Nathan Glazer are among the contributors.

Grant, Carl A., ed. *Multicultural Education: Commitments, Issues and Applications.* Washington, D.C.: Association for Supervision and Curriculum Development, 1977.

Broadly defining multicultural education, this book includes articles on ethnic groups, student rights, sexism, and the educational dimensions of cultural diversity.

Grove, Cornelius Lee. *Communications Across Cultures: A Report on Cross-Cultural Research.* Washington, D.C.: National Education Association, 1976.

The problems involved in communicating across cultures and the findings of cross-cultural research are some of the important topics discussed in this monograph.

Guide for Multicultural Education: Content and Context. Sacramento, Calif.: California State Department of Education, 1977.

This book contains an excellent instrument which can be used for evaluating and selecting materials that reflect ethnic and cultural diversity.

Hansen-Krening, Nancy. *Competency and Creativity in Language Arts: A Multiethnic Focus.* Reading, Mass.: Addison-Wesley, 1979.

Written for both pre-service and in-service teachers, this book combines theory and practice in integrating multiethnic awareness and education into the teaching of basic communication skills. It is designed to teach basic language arts skills while expanding ethnic literacy.

Herman, Judith, ed. *The Schools and Group Identity.* New York: American Jewish Committee, 1974.

This highly acclaimed monograph on the "new pluralism" was stimulated by the ethnic revitalization movements of the 1960's and 1970's.

King, Edith W. *Teaching Ethnic Awareness: Methods and Materials for the Elementary School.* Santa Monica, Calif.: Goodyear, 1980.

This resource book for elementary school teachers is divided into three major parts: Background for the Teacher in Multiethnic Education, Activities for the Multiethnic Elementary School, and Resources for the Multiethnic Teacher.

Klassen, Frank H., and Gollnick, Donna M., eds. *Pluralism and the American Teacher: Issues and Case Studies.* Washington, D.C.: American Association of Colleges for Teacher Education, 1977.

James A. Banks, Geneva Gay, Harry N. Rivlin, Carl A. Grant, and other specialists in multiethnic and multicultural education discuss ways in which teacher education can and should become more sensitive to the ethnic diversity in American life and culture.

Labov, William. *The Study of Nonstandard English.* Urbana, Ill.: National Council of Teachers of English, 1969.

This monograph is a well-researched and thoughtful discussion of nonstandard English. Black English is one of the important topics treated.

Miel, Alice, with Edwin Kiester, Jr. *The Shortchanged Children of Suburbia.* New York: American Jewish Committee, 1967.

A seminal but often neglected study, this work documents the extent to which children in suburban areas are often isolated from racial, religious, and social class differences.

Noar, Gertrude. *The Teacher and Integration.* Rev. ed. Washington, D.C.: National Education Association, 1974.

The author draws upon her many years of rich experiences to pose and respond to questions that teachers in integrated schools are likely to ask and want answered.

Novak, Michael. *Further Reflections on Ethnicity.* Middletown, Penn.: Jednota Press, 1977.

This brilliant and thoughtful book discusses the "new pluralism." Although Novak focuses on White ethnic groups, many of his observations can help the teacher to understand all ethnic groups in the United States.

Pedersen, Paul; Lonner, Walter J.; and Draguns, Juris G., eds. *Counseling Across Cultures.* Honolulu, Hawaii: University Press of Hawaii, 1976.

This excellent and well-researched collection of original essays discusses issues related to cross-cultural counseling.

Ramírez, Manuel III and Castañeda, Alfredo. *Cultural Democracy, Bicognitive Development and Education.* New York: Academic Press, 1974.

This seminal book presents theory and research findings related to the cognitive styles of Mexican-American and Anglo youths, with important implications for the schooling of minority students.

Saville-Troike, Muriel. *Foundations for Teaching English as a Second Language: Theory and Method for Multicultural Education.* Englewood Cliffs, N.J.: Prentice-Hall, 1976.

This book discusses the psychological, linguistic, and cultural foundations of teaching English as a second language, as well as strategies for instruction and preparing for teaching in the multicultural classroom.

Saville-Troike, Muriel and Troike, Rudolph C. *A Handbook of Bilingual Education.* Rev. ed. Washington, D.C.: Teachers of English to Speakers of Other Languages, 1971.

This introductory book on bilingual education discusses various aspects of bilingual education, including rationale, design, languages of instruction, pedagogical considerations, and evaluation.

Stewart, Edward C. *American Cultural Patterns: A Cross-Cultural Perspective.* LaGrange Park, Ill.: Intercultural Network, Inc. 1972.

The author discusses some of the basic values and characteristics shared by all Americans, regardless of ethnic group.

Trueba, Henry T. and Barnett-Mizrahi, Carol, eds. *Bilingual Multicultural Education and the Professional: From Theory to Practice.* Rowley, Mass.: Newbury House Publishers, 1979.

This collection includes many essays reprinted from other sources. Among the contributors are Joshua A. Fishman and Muriel Saville-Troike.

Weinberg, Meyer. *A Chance to Learn: A History of Race and Education in the United States.* New York: Cambridge University Press, 1977.

Written by a veteran in the multiethnic education field, this book chronicles the educational history of Afro-Americans, Mexican-Americans, American Indians, and Puerto Rican-Americans.

The Contributors

TOMÁS A. ARCINIEGA is Dean of the College of Education at San Diego State University. A former intermediate grade and secondary school teacher, Dr. Arciniega has written extensively on the educational problems of minority groups. His publications include *American Education and the Hispanic: A Review of Current Issues and Concerns, Preparing Teachers of Mexican-Americans: A Sociocultural and Political Issue,* and *Chicanos and Native Americans: The Territorial Minorities.*

GWENDOLYN C. BAKER is Chief, Minorities and Women's Programs, National Institute of Education. Dr. Baker is a former elementary teacher in the Ann Arbor (Michigan) Public Schools; and has been a professor at the University of Michigan. She is the co-editor of *Teaching in a Multicultural Society* and *Multicultural Education: Teaching About Minority Women.*

CHERRY A. BANKS is a counselor and a consultant in Seattle, Washington. She is the author of "A Content Analysis of the Treatment of Black Americans on Television," *Social Education* (April 1977), and co-author of *March Toward Freedom: A History of Black Americans.* In her graduate degree program at Seattle University, she specialized in community college counseling. Her current research and training interest is cross-cultural counseling. Ms. Banks has served as a consultant to a number of educational and professional organizations, including the University of Washington, Seattle University, and the American Library Association.

JAMES A. BANKS is Professor of Education at the University of Washington and Vice-President of the National Council for the Social Studies. He will serve as President-Elect of the Council in 1981 and as President in 1982. Professor Banks is a specialist in social studies education and multiethnic education. His books include *Teaching Strategies for the Social Studies, Teaching Strategies for Ethnic Studies, Teaching Ethnic Studies: Concepts and Strategies, Black Self-Concept: Implications for Education and Social Science,* and *Multiethnic Education: Theory and Practice.* In 1973 Professor Banks was awarded a Spencer Fellowship by the National Academy of Education, and in 1980 he was awarded fellowships from the Kellogg and Rockefeller Foundations.

ELEANOR BLUMENBERG is National Education Director, Anti-Defamation League of B'nai B'rith, New York. Dr. Blumenberg frequently serves as a consultant to school systems, professional organizations, government agencies, and private industry on problems in intergroup relations and conflict resolution. She has contributed to numerous journals and to the book, *Racism and Sexism: Responding to the Challenge.* Dr. Blumenberg has taught at the University of Southern California and at other universities.

EMILY BRIZENDINE is a Multicultural Education Program Specialist with the Long Beach (California) Unified School District. She received her bachelor's and master's degrees from the University of California, Los Angeles, and is currently a doctoral candidate in Administrative Policy Studies in Education at UCLA. A former high school social studies teacher, Ms. Brizendine has been an Instructor of Asian-American Studies at California State University, Long Beach, and a Congressional Intern with the United States House of Representatives.

CHARLES W. CHENG received his doctoral degree from the Graduate School of Education, Harvard University. An Assistant Professor of Education at the University of California, Los Angeles, when his untimely death occurred in 1979, Professor Cheng did extensive work on parent and community participation in education and was working on leadership theory and multiethnic education. He is the author of *Altering Collective Bargaining: Citizen Participation in Educational Decision-Making.*

CARLOS E. CORTÉS is Professor of History at the University of California, Riverside, and past chair of Chicano Studies. Among his publications are *Three Perspectives on Ethnicity: Blacks, Chicanos, and Native Americans, Understanding You and Them: Tips for Teaching about Ethnicity,* and *Gaucho Politics in Brazil.* He has edited two major book series, *The Mexican American* (21 volumes) and *The Chicano Heritage* (55 volumes). Dr. Cortes has lectured widely throughout the United States on such topics as Latin American and Chicano history, Chicano culture, social studies education, multicultural education, and film-and-history.

BARBARA G. COX is Co-Director of the Bilingual Preschool Project and Associate Director of the Follow Through Project at the University of California, Santa Cruz. Ms. Cox has developed curriculum materials for a bilingual curriculum in mathematics, reading, science, and cultural studies. Her papers include "Assessing Biculturalism in Mexican-American College Students." and "Parent-Child Verbal Interactions: A Mexican-American Case Study."

WALTER CURRIE is Assistant Director of the newly created Gabriel Dumont Institute of Native Studies and Applied Research in Regina, Saskatchewan. A former elementary school teacher and principal, he spent the 1975–76 academic year at the Center for Indian Education at Arizona State University where he did work on the education of American Indian students. Dr. Currie participated in the Ninth Annual National Indian Education Convention in St. Paul, Minnesota, in 1977, where he presented a paper entitled "American Indian Post-Secondary Education: Needs of Indian Students and How They Should Be Met." He also presented a paper at the First Annual American Indian Studies Seminar, California State University, North Ridge, in 1978.

GENEVA GAY is Associate Professor of Education at Purdue University. She has contributed chapters to a number of books, including *Teaching Ethnic Studies: Concepts and Strategies, Language and Cultural Diversity in American Education, Teaching American History: The Quest for Relevancy, Multicultural Education: Commitments, Issues and Applications,* and *Pluralism and the American Teacher: Issues and Case Studies.*

CARL A. GRANT is Associate Professor of Curriculum and Instruction at the University of Wisconsin, Madison. He is the editor of *In Praise of Diversity: A Resource Book for Multicultural Education, Multicultural Education: Definition, Issues, and Applications,* and *Community Participation in Education.* Professor Grant is the co-author of *Realities, Roles, and Rites of Passage: An Introduction to Teaching.*

GARY R. HOWARD is Director of the Multicultural Education Project in the Arlington (Washington) School District. A graduate of Yale University, where he co-authored a research study published in the *Journal of Applied Social Psychology,* he wrote his master's thesis at Western Washington University on multicultural education. Mr. Howard trains teachers in multicultural education in the Arlington School District.

JANE R. MERCER is Professor of Sociology at the University of California, Riverside. She has contributed chapters to many books including *The Mentally Retarded Child and His Family; Race, Change, and Urban Society;*

Patients, Physicians, and Illnesses; The Fallacy of IQ; Uses of the Sociology of Education; and *The Testing of Black Students.* She is the author of *Labeling the Mentally Retarded.*

JEANNIE OAKES is Research Associate, Research Division, Institute for Development of Educational Activities, Inc., Los Angeles. Dr. Oakes received her M.A. in American Studies from California State University (Los Angeles) and her Ph.D. from the University of California, Los Angeles. She is a former secondary English teacher in the Glendora (California) School District.

MANUEL RAMÍREZ III is Professor of Psychology, Director of the Follow Through Project, and Co-Director of the Bilingual Preschool Project at the University of California, Santa Cruz. He has contributed chapters to a number of books, including *Views Across the Border: The United States and Mexico, Community Psychology in Transition,* and *Chicano Psychology.* He is the co-author of *Cultural Democracy, Bicognitive Development and Education, Mexican-Americans and Educational Change,* and *Bilingual Education in the United States.*

MURIEL SAVILLE-TROIKE is Associate Professor of Linguistics at Georgetown University, Washington, D.C. Her books and monographs include *A Guide to Culture in the Classroom, Foundations for Teaching English as a Second Language, Bilingual Children, A Handbook of Bilingual Education,* and *The Ethnography of Communication.* A former kindergarten teacher, Professor Saville-Troike has contributed chapters to a number of books including *Multicultural Education: Definitions, Issues and Applications, Reading for the Disadvantaged, International Perspectives on Bilingual Education,* and *Discovering Language with Children.*

BARBARA J. SHIN is a teacher at the Pratt Continuous Progress Elementary School in the Minneapolis (Minnesota) Public Schools, and is Chairperson of the Minnesota Education Association Human Relations Commission. A leader in human relations in-service education, she frequently conducts school district workshops in communication skills, community involvement, conflict management, and cross-cultural education. In 1971, she was named an "Outstanding Young Woman of America." In 1975, she was recognized for "Dedicated Service" as a Human Relations Coordinator by the Minneapolis Public Schools. In 1978, she was named the "Outstanding Woman Leader" by the Minnesota Education Association. And in 1979, Ms. Shin was awarded an H. Councill Trenholm Memorial Award by the National Education Association for her leadership in human relations education.